BORN TO FLY

SQUADRON LEADER NORMAN ROSE
AFC & BAR AMN RAF(Retd)

BORN TO FLY

SQUADRON LEADER NORMAN ROSE

AFC & BAR AMN RAF(Retd)

THE AUTOBIOGRAPHY OF A RAF PILOT
WHO FLEW MILITARY AIRCRAFT IN WWII AND
THROUGHOUT THE COLD WAR ERA,
1942 TO 1989

Keyham Books

©Norman Rose

First published in 2005
by
Keyham Books
Startley
Chippenham SN15 5HG

www.keyhambooks.co.uk

All rights reserved
Unauthorised publication
contravenes existing laws

ISBN: 0 9527715 8 6

Set in Verdana and Times New Roman by Keyham Books
Printed and bound by Antony Rowe Ltd

CONTENTS

PREFACE 1
ACKNOWLEDGEMENTS 3
FOREWORD 5
1. JOINING UP - 1942 9
2. TRAINING TO BE A PILOT 1942-1944 11
3. TO WAR WITH THE HURRICANE IN ITALY 23
4. BACK TO PALESTINE 1945-46 29
5. THE EARLY JETS 1946-48 37
6. OCU INSTRUCTOR 1948 47
7. CFS AND 6 FTS - 1948-50 51
8. THE FERRY TRAINING UNIT - 1950 - 1952 61
9. THE OVERSEAS FERRY UNIT 1952- 1954 69
10. OCTU & THE FAR EAST - JET CONVERSIONS 1954 - 1957 83
11. TEST PILOT 1957 - 1960 97
12. THE WHISPERING GIANT - 1960 - 1963 105
13. OPERATION VANTAGE - 1961 (KUWAIT THE FIRST TIME) 111
14. 'NEDDIES BAR' AND LIFE IN BERLIN - 1962 117
15. FLYING VIPs and TROUBLE IN BEIRUT 123
16. THE FREIGHT HOLD FIRE - NOV. 1962 131
17. THE SAGA OF THE RUNAWAY PROPELLER - DEC. 1962 135
18. SOME WEATHER HAZARDS OF THE INDIAN OCEAN 143
19. THE ROYAL MALAYSIAN AIR FORCE 1963 - 66 149
20. THE HERALD AT WAR - 1963-66 157
21. A ROYAL FLIGHT AND A MEDIVAC 161
22. AVM 'JOHNNIE' JOHNSON AND A BASSET HOUND 165
23. CONFRONTATION - BEING SHOT AT DROPPING LEAFLETS 169
24. ASYMMETRIC FLAP OVER KUALA LUMPUR 173
25. BACK TO BRITANNIAS - TRIBULATIONS OF A 'TRUCKIE' 179
26. 'AUNTIE FLOW' 1971 - 1973 191
27. HONG KONG APPROACHES AND GANDER WEATHER 201
28. THE PAKISTAN AIR LIFT 205
29. THE GURKHA AIRLIFT FROM HONG KONG 209
30. THE CYPRUS EMERGENCY 217
31. 10,000 HOURS AND FAREWELL TO THE BRITANNIA 221
32. BOSCOMBE DOWN AND TWO 55TH BIRTHDAYS 1979 229
33. LIFE ON THE AIR EXPERIENCE FLIGHT - 1979-89 235
APPENDIX 1 - SOME PERSONAL PHOTOS 243
APPENDIX 2 - AIRCRAFT MODELS 253

> My memoirs in this book are
> dedicated to my family
> and for posterity.

PREFACE
by Simon Gifford

In this book Norman Rose describes his record-breaking career with the Royal Air Force, during which he flew almost continuously from his first tentative flights aged 18 till retiring at 65. From flying rocket-firing Hurricanes in the Balkans and the skies over a troubled Palestine, to introducing future generations to the joys of flying with the Air Experience Flight, his story is remarkable in illustrating one man's desire to stay where he belonged - in the cockpit.

Within these pages, Norman describes some of the varied incidents that occurred whilst carrying out a variety of jobs: fighter pilot, instructor, ferry pilot, test pilot and 'truckie'. Whilst carrying out these differing jobs he flew many of the significant types in service and also a few 'weird-and-wonderful' aircraft as well.

Throughout his career he was decorated three times with two AFCs and an AMN. He was also awarded two 'Green Endorsements' for exceptional flying skill and judgement by saving two aircraft from crashing and has several valedictory commendations. After he retired he was awarded two further honours - in 1993 his longevity as an RAF pilot became an entry in the Guinness Book of Records and then in 2000 he was honoured by the Guild of Air Pilots and Navigators (GAPAN) and made a 'Master Air Pilot '.

Only 810 of these honours have been made in the 71 years of GAPAN's existence. The award (signed and presented by Prince Philip, Duke of Edinburgh) is made to a pilot who has displayed exceptional qualities of pilotage, airmanship and character but is also in recognition of meritorious service consistent with high standards in professional flying, which has brought honour and respect to the aviation profession.

Many stories have been written about wartime exploits, but

only a few about peacetime flying throughout the 'Cold War' period and after. This book is a welcome addition in describing less well-known and unpublicised aspects of the Royal Air Force's peacetime flying. However, life in the Services was not always a bed of roses and Norman also usefully describes some of the personal stresses and strains that members of the RAF accept as part of their service.

On a personal level, I first spoke to Norman whilst researching No.6 Squadron's operations in Palestine after the end of the war. His generosity of spirit in helping a stranger with a somewhat unusual request amply illustrated the enthusiasm he still has for the world of flying. In writing this book, Norman describes a career that is both inspiring and colourful and I believe that it is no exaggeration to say that he was '*Born to Fly*'.

ACKNOWLEDGEMENTS

To: Vivienne Lelliott - for her patience and understanding in the very long and onerous task of typing up the undecipherable scribble of the manuscript and for teaching me the proper way to operate my computer. She taught me how to collate the work and present it in a readable form for a book.

To: Simon Gifford - for giving so much of his valuable time proof-reading the document, and advising on its layout for printing. He gave me the much-valued benefit of his experience as an author.

To: Tom Walls - for first influencing me to write all my memoirs down on paper. He was an instructor at RAF Woodvale when I was CO of No.10 Air Experience Flight and he convinced me then, and has since, that my story should be told.

To: My Wife Shirley - for her understanding and patience with my long absences on the computer while writing this book!

To: My Son - for helping me with an in-depth and detailed critique in the early stages of the manuscript and who was responsible for recommending I should change the style to an autobiography.

... and finally to Squadron Leader David Berry - a fellow Britannia pilot and long standing friend, compatriot and in retirement an author/publisher in his own right - for his most generous offer to finalise and publish my memoirs for posterity on my behalf.

FOREWORD

An essay written by the 17-year old Air Cadet in 1941 on his return from ATC camp at RAF Halton Buckinghamshire.

My First Flight

It was raining heavily beating on our faces as we marched. We were four in number, about to fly for the first time and quite naturally excited although we all tried to hide it. As the aerodrome came in sight we forgot the rain and our eyes searched for a likely looking aircraft. There were Wellingtons, Blenheims and Tiger Moths; we hoped the flight would be in the Moths. We marched to the front of the hangars and were met by a Flight Lieutenant who bore the ribbon of the DFC on his breast. He told us he was to pilot us in an Airspeed Envoy which once belonged to the Royal Flight and which lay at rest on the tarmac. I experienced slight regret at this as I had badly wanted to fly in a military aircraft but, after all, I decided, it did not matter so long as I actually flew.

Before we climbed in, we were given last minute instructions from the pilot about such matters as being sick in the air, not to walk around while in flight and to observe what we could from the air. He told us we were not going to have parachutes at which visions of engine failure in mid-air swept across my mind, though they seemed small troubles compared with the excitement of the moment.

We closely inspected the machine as soon as we were inside. The King used it in the days of peace and plenty, for it was truly magnificent, with soft red plush seats, curtained windows and all the modern devices of comfort. I was not the lucky person to sit up by the pilot so, as the 'drome had a left hand circuit, I made the best of what I had by sitting myself on the left hand side of the machine so that I could look down when we banked. The engines revved and we taxied away to the far end of the field where we turned and stopped while the pilot made a careful check on everything, revving first one engine, then the other. A swift, gentle, turn of a little wheel down by the pilot's side corrected the 'tail trim'. Then the engines began to roar in earnest and the 'plane bumped forward across the grass towards the distant hangar, gathering speed until it became almost frightening. Those hangars simply seemed to leap towards us. The bumping ceased suddenly and we knew we were airborne. I wondered whether we were going to hit the hangars. They, however, passed just below us. I gave a slight breath of relief and my muscles relaxed.

I began to look about me, memorising where the aerodrome was, noting features and landmarks near it, and watching the pilot's actions up at the front. The rain had stopped temporarily so I was able to scan the ground quite clearly while we climbed. When we were about 500 feet up I became conscious of a queer sensation of rising and falling giving me a funny feeling in the pit of my stomach. We banked suddenly and I realised the materialisation of an ambition - I was flying - separate from the world below in a universe of my own. It was really exhilarating, sitting there looking through the window to see the earth spread below me. Cloud ceiling was at 1000 feet, which we had now reached and streaked into for a few seconds at a time.

Grey wisps of cloud flashed past the windows. Rising and falling, termed 'bumping' I believe, now became very noticeable and I gripped the sides of my seat every time we dropped. It started to rain again driving against the Perspex at the front. Strangely enough there was a window open at the front but no rain came in! We banked again, more sharply this time, the sensation is indescribable, and I began to concentrate on more serious things, other than glorying in the situation, such as map reading and trying to remember in which direction the airfield lay, compared with the direction in which the 'plane was facing.

We lost height steadily until we circled at about 300 or 400 feet round the aerodrome and then banked so that we faced the hangars just as we did when we took off. The engines stopped and the noise of rushing air sounded eerie, we were losing height rapidly, and very rapidly I thought, in fact the ground seemed to race towards us and I felt an urge to yell to the pilot to pull out. I experienced a pressure on my eardrums as we raced downwards. The ground was very near now but we flattened out just in time, the grass streaked past, almost near enough to lean out and touch.

Suddenly the engines burst into life again, the pilot turned and grinned at us, and we sped across the field, climbed up and away, circled again and this time we approached from a much lower height. I knew we were going to land this time because the chap sitting up beside the pilot pumped the undercarriage down. We came in a lot slower, the engines stopped and the 'props' ticked over, the sound of rushing wind became loud in my ears. Again I experienced the sensation of pressure on my eardrums. I glanced out along the wings to see if the flaps were down and they were. I felt safe this time. About 20 feet off the ground my heart jumped because we dropped rather alarmingly to within about six feet of the grass. However, a perfect landing was accomplished but the moment we touched down could not be ascertained exactly by any of us.

We taxied over to the hangars and the flight was over. I had one lingering glance round and jumped out. What a pity it was over, how I would like it all over again! We went over to the pilot, thanked him, and asked him if he meant to scare us or whether he actually intended to land when we came in the first time. The answer he gave us was, 'Well, what do you think?'

As we marched away, I, full of thoughts of this my first flight, realised to the full the feelings of being above the ground and I look forward eagerly to the day when I can take over the controls, and (with the 'Wings' of a pilot of the RAF on my chest), take off and, like a bird - FLY.

No.97 Cpl. N. E. Rose,
No.1044 (Banstead) Squadron, ATC

Chapter 1
JOINING UP - 1942

I was born on the 30th May 1924 on a farm at Wisborough Green in Sussex, the son of a farmer. I grew up with my two sisters in a very old farmhouse that was mentioned in the Doomsday Book. When I was six years old, my family moved to No.60 Wickham Avenue, Bexhill-on-Sea in East Sussex.

In 1936 my family took up residence in Walton-on-the-Hill near Epsom Downs. I was educated at Reigate Grammar School until 1941. When I left school I worked for a short time at Costains, the building firm, as a costing clerk but I hated the job and became determined to volunteer for the Royal Air Force.

In the summer of 1940 when the Battle of Britain was

My two sisters, Marjorie and Eileen, and Mum and Dad.

at its height, I used to sit out on Walton Heath and watch the dogfights overhead and I dreamed of becoming a pilot. As soon as the Air Training Corps (ATC) was set up in 1941, I was one of the first to join as a founder member. I used to pedal my bicycle eight miles each way, to my nearest unit at Banstead, two or three times a week attending lectures and parades.

I worked hard for every possible proficiency badge I could obtain and by the time I left to join the RAF had been promoted to the ('exalted'!) rank of Corporal! My education had been disrupted in 1940 because my school went on to half days. The building had to be shared with other schools that had been bombed out in London and so I was unable to take my Matriculation Examinations (today they are the GCSE exams). However, I was not academically bright, as my school reports confirm, and I was bored with school lessons so perhaps it was not all the school's fault! I became quite fanatical in my determination to join the RAF and when I went to RAF Cardington for my interviews and tests for aircrew, I knew that my weakest point was going to be my lack of academic qualifications. It was made clear to me that only my commendable results obtained at my ATC Squadron swayed the board to accept me. In fact, of the 100 or so applicants at Cardington with me, only eight young men were accepted for pilot training.

The real highlight of my time with 1044 (Banstead) Squadron ATC was my very first flight in an aeroplane at RAF Halton in the summer of 1941, and I was moved to write an essay about it for school work as soon as I got home and I have reproduced it word for word in the Foreword to this book.

After my interviews and selection, I was sent home to wait. The days dragged on and it seemed an eternity before the buff coloured OHMS envelope dropped through the letterbox. I was so excited I burst a blood vessel in my nose!

Chapter 2
TRAINING TO BE A PILOT 1942-1944

I enlisted in the Royal Air Force on 17th August 1942 as 1627339 Aircraftman Second Class Rose N.E. In October I reported to the Aircrew Reception Centre at St. Johns Wood in London, known to us budding young aircrews as 'ACRC', where we were kitted out with uniforms and flying kit. We drilled daily in Regents Park and were given elementary lessons about the Royal Air Force. The daily routine meant rising at 6.00am, marching in the dark to London Zoo for breakfast where we queued beside the Zoo restaurant beneath a huge monkey cage. The man at the front of the marchers carried a white light and the rear man, 50 ranks behind, carried a red light; all marched at 140 paces per minute. Even the Sick Parade from Viceroy Court to Abbey Lodge Sick Quarters, a distance of two miles, was done at this terrible pace. Reporting sick was purgatory, having to put on full uniform, including greatcoat, backpack, water bottle, side pack, webbing, gas mask, gas cape, and tin helmet. With that load about their person and at such a crippling pace, it put off many malingerers!

I recall pay parades with a certain amount of nostalgia, queuing up at Lords Cricket Ground once a fortnight to receive 10 shillings, (50p). Like most young *ab initio* airmen, I received a week's 'jankers' (punishment) for being late back from a weekend at home. It made precious little difference to my Commanding Officer that it was foggy and not my fault. He just did not believe my tale!

On another occasion I was awarded seven days cookhouse fatigues for telling the Flight Sergeant I was agnostic after dodging a Sunday morning church parade. When the Flight Sergeant asked me what an agnostic was I did not know! A 'worldly' airman, who shared my room and was re-mustering from groundcrew to aircrew, had advised me to say it! However I enjoyed this chore because it got me out of early morning Physical Training, Arms Drill, Parades and many other onerous duties. It was shift work, which meant plenty of time off, and I had fun with the WAAF's (Women's Auxiliary Air Force) in London Zoo's cookhouse!

After two months at ACRC I moved to No.3 Personnel Despatch Centre in Blackpool. I waited there to be sent off to 'somewhere' for my flying training. I spent three weeks being drilled on the seafront and getting kitted out for overseas. I lived in a boarding house in relative comfort looked after by a strict and volatile Blackpool landlady. The evenings were spent in the Winter Gardens or the Tower Ballroom dancing, drinking beer with my friends and chatting up the Blackpool girls!

At the end of my three weeks I was shepherded into a blacked-out train at about 3.15 in the afternoon at Blackpool station. The train arrived at Liverpool Lime Street the next afternoon! Anyone who knows his geography will know that it is only 1 hour and 30 minutes at the most from Blackpool to Liverpool by train. There were many theories advanced throughout that long night as to why the journey was taking so long. Many were convinced the train had gone through Crewe to London and back again but this was never really confirmed. If the object of it all had been to fool any German spies, it was shattered that afternoon when my batch marched through the centre of Liverpool to the docks dressed in full webbing, greatcoats, packs etc. and on top for all the world to see was perched our tropical topees!

The '*Dominion Monarch*' sailed from Greenock into a typical January, North Atlantic gale. I immediately went green and departed into a dark hole somewhere in the bowels of the ship to lie down. I felt so awful I was convinced I was going to die, and more to the point, wished I could! It was five days later when a pale and

'*Dominion Monarch*'

thinner apparition emerged to look at the light of day after the gale had abated and the ship was steadier! Five weeks later we steamed slowly into Durban harbour. Everyone on the ship was overcome with pride and emotion when they saw and heard a lady dressed completely in white singing patriotic songs like '*Land of Hope and Glory*' through a megaphone from the jetty. This famous lady, Perla Siedle Gibson, met all the Allied ships coming into Durban throughout the war. Her welcoming gesture was always much appreciated by the soldiers, sailors and airmen on the ships. The next stop was Durban's Clairwood Transit Camp for an unforgettable four weeks. We lived in stables not long vacated by the original inmates and slept on concrete floors. Some nights we stood guard next to a snake-infested sugar plantation supposedly as part of our training and indoctrination to the Royal Air Force overseas - or so we were told! It was probably the Air Force's misguided way of establishing whether we budding young pilots had the necessary courage, determination and character to fly aeroplanes in the face of wartime adversity! One wonders!

    I found these guard duties very scary standing in the still

balmy nights holding a rifle and listening for the faintest rustle in the blackness. Having had no experience of life outside Britain, all we young hopefuls listened fearfully to blood curdling tales of previous intakes dying like flies from snakebites! We all wrapped newspaper thickly round our legs and stood quaking through the long nights praying for daybreak - and we hadn't a clue what we were supposed to be guarding!

During daytime we attended lectures on the Royal Air Force in general, given by an over enthusiastic Drill Sergeant. This Non-Commissioned Officer talked to us at great length on the dimensions of the RAF ensign, what would happen to us in Southern Rhodesia and how he thought aeroplanes should be flown! He probably hadn't even been near an aeroplane in his life!

We were drilled mercilessly in the South African sun. I

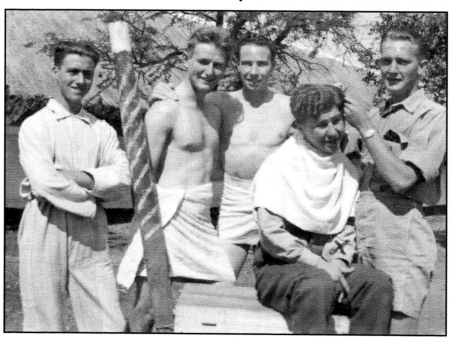

Sunday morning ritual - haircuts by other cadets at ITW Hillside.

remember vividly how one poor cadet died of peritonitis because the permanent staff would not believe he was ill. They thought he was shamming to get out of the infamous guard duty. The young lad came off duty finally one day in a state of collapse and crying with pain. Despite efforts to get medical help it was too late; he was taken to hospital where he died of the peritonitis soon after arrival.

However, life at Clairwood Camp did have its compensations. We had as much milk, eggs and fruit as we could eat. It was a marvellous luxury to us having come from a very spartan Britain where everything was on ration and in short supply. Our days off were spent in Durban with lots of hospitality from the South Africans and many sincere friendships were struck up. One aspect of life there I abhorred was the way the whites treated the blacks. For example, they would not let them mix in the towns and would actually kick them off the sidewalk and only allow them to sit in the back four seats upstairs on a bus. Inevitably, my stay in Durban came to an end, goodbyes were said and we young trainees sadly boarded a train to Bulawayo in Southern Rhodesia (now called Zimbabwe) and arrived at our Initial Training Wing at Hillside.

The ITW proved to be 14 weeks of real hard classroom graft as so much had to be absorbed in a very short time. I wasn't blessed with a photographic mind and I had to sit down every night learning off by heart most of the day's teaching. While I was doing this, the brighter boys went into Bulawayo for the evening. I drove myself hard because I knew that what I was doing now could turn out to be the foundation stone for my future - how right I was! However at weekends I relaxed a little and went into town with my fellow cadets to survey the local Rhodesian girls and let my hair down with them. The hangovers from an over indulgence of South African brandy were very much in evidence on the parade ground on Sunday mornings with almost every other face a ghastly green!

After ITW I was posted to No.26 Elementary Flying Training School at Guinea Fowl near Gwelo. It was equipped with Tiger Moths and my very first flight in one became seared on my mind forever. It was probably the psychological cause of my future dislike of being upside down and spinning. Spinning always 'toppled my gyro'

Model of a Tiger Moth. With retirement I started making scale models of every aeroplane I had flown in my 47 years as a RAF pilot. Each of the 72 models is crafted in their authentic colour schemes with the actual airframe registrations and squadron code letters.

and invariably made me sick. My instructor was a bright young Scotsman who had been 'creamed off' at the end of his training to be a flying instructor, whereas he wanted to go and fly Spitfires! My

Self in cockpit of Harvard at No.6 FTS Ternhill.

straps were not checked by him before we took off so they were not as tight as they should have been. So on this, my very first flight, I became extremely frightened when he inverted the Tiger Moth without warning so that I was hanging upside down, my face out in the slipstream, legs hanging down (up!) in the cockpit and blood rushing to my head. He then subjected me to a prolonged session of aerobatics and a long spin and I was very, very sick! If this young man was trying to impress me, or just venting his frustration, will probably never be known. However, I eventually overcame my fright and psychological flaw and flew my first solo in the Tiger Moth after nine hours - a thrilling moment I have never forgotten.

Just as a matter of interest, Ian Smith, who became Prime Minister of Rhodesia, had just preceded me through my flying schools.

Having successfully completed the EFTS, I moved on to flying Harvards at No.22 Service Flying Training School at Thornhill. I think it was only in the Southern Rhodesian Air Training Group that this happened, but we were all promoted to 'Acting Sgt Unpaid' and lived in a form of unheard of (for cadet pilots) luxury and 'waited on' in the Sgts' Mess. This also meant we lived two to a room with a 'Boy' (ours was named 'Sixpence'!) to clean and make the beds as compared to our existence at the EFTS where we were living ten to

North American Harvard trainer.

No.22 SFTS, Thornhill, Southern Rhodesia, Course 37A. I am 5th from the right, front row.

15 in a block with all the accompanying 'bull'! I certainly found a big difference between the Tiger Moth and the Harvard. Eventually the great day came, five months later, when I was presented with my coveted 'Wings'. I think every pilot will tell you that secretly it is the proudest day of their lives. Everything I had striven for was fulfilled. I was bursting with so much pride when those wings were pinned on. I don't think there has ever been a young pilot who hasn't secretly admired his left breast afterwards in the mirror!

After a well-earned leave spent at Meikles Hotel in Salisbury, I was on my way to the Middle East. The journey north took me by train through what is now Zambia (it was Northern Rhodesia then), and I was then transferred to a 3-ton truck through the Congo (now Zaire) to Kisumu, Kenya. At Kisumu I boarded a BOAC Lockheed Lodestar bound for Khartoum via Juba and Malakal. After two nights in Khartoum, I then boarded a BOAC Empire Flying Boat, the *'Cambria'*, and splashed down on the Nile in Cairo. These days it would cost an arm and a leg to do a trip like that as a tourist.

The next six weeks were spent at the 'Middle East Aircrew Reception Centre' in Heliopolis, Egypt. I was accommodated in the bare and requisitioned Heliopolis Palace Hotel where I immediately had a massive three cubic centimetres injection for Bubonic Plague - an experience I will never forget! The doctor's *modus operandi* was to attack the poor unfortunate's bottom with a resounding slap and at the same time thrust the huge needle in. The recipient didn't know which was more painful, the needle or the slap. Within an hour I was laid out on my bed wondering which was worse, the effects of the vaccine or actually having the plague; I felt terrible!

Apart from the normal collection of inoculations dished out to servicemen in Egypt, we young pilots were warned that anyone falling into the 'Sweetwater Canal' at Ismailia would receive a 'full house' of injections - the mind boggles to think of what that consisted! The 'Sweetwater Canal' was a very large foul, smelly open sewer used by the locals as a toilet and for disposal of sewage and drains.

I then moved on to No.71 Operational Training Unit Ismailia, in the Suez Canal Zone, which was equipped with Hurricanes. We sat in hot classrooms for the first two weeks learning all about the Hurricane from end to end. Each pilot was then given three dual refresher flights in a Harvard and then sent off in a Hurricane on his own - not knowing what to expect or whether he would be able to cope. It was made worse in my case because my instructor was a Greek Flying Officer called Xydis, who had very limited English. I had no Greek, so my pre-flight briefing was a bit limited to say the least!

A first solo could always be recognised by the pitching gyrations of the Hurricane immediately after take-off. There was only one lever to operate both the undercarriage and flaps in a 'H' form of

Another Harvard model.

slots. To select the undercarriage up entailed pushing the lever up into the left slot and similarly to select the flaps up the lever is moved up the right hand slot of the 'H', the opposite being 'down' selections. This lever was positioned down on the right hand side of the cockpit beside the pilot's right knee. On take-off the pilot had his left hand on the throttle lever and his right hand on the control column. To raise the undercarriage after take-off meant a change of hands, i.e. left hand to the control column ('the stick') with the right hand reaching down to the undercarriage lever. Reaching down, for those with short arms like me, also involved leaning forward. This tended to inadvertently push the 'stick' forward, which inevitably pushed the nose down requiring a very hasty correction to pull the 'stick' back! Until the pilot got used to these contortions, the Hurricane would seesaw into the distance! Wartime pilots would never admit it but their first solo in a powerful and fast operational aeroplane, without dual instruction first and with very few flying hours, was a great milestone and quite a hazardous experience especially when they were so young and inexperienced.

    The airmen and off-duty pilots at the Operational Training Unit were permitted to gather at the end of the runway to watch the first solo pantomime as the pupil pilots launched themselves into the air and then tried to put their Hurricanes back on the ground for the first time! These first solos were normally saved until Saturday mornings to amuse the ground crews but, of course, the worried and petrified instructors also gathered, fingers crossed, to watch their prodigies. If a Hurricane was 'held off' too high on landing it stalled, dropped a wing and scraped it on the runway. This resulted in sparks emitting from the wing tip and was often followed by an uncontrolled swing off the runway into the sand. Many of us desperately opened up with a great burst of engine power and overshot to go round again as we poor frightened pupils realised we were stalling or were too high or too fast. Some even forgot to lower their undercarriage in the melee, making the demented runway controller fire off red Very cartridges one after another at them, as they approached the runway. Others got desperate after many aborted attempts and decided 'to hell with it' and stayed down in very 'dodgy' arrivals bordering on near 'prangs'! The Ismailia runway was wide but not very long and those who came in too fast and decided to stay down would run into the sand at the end of the runway, tip up on their nose and break the propeller. These sorts of incidents were accepted as part of the learning process in those days because of the inexperience of the young pilots and the lack of a dual controlled aircraft with an instructor.

It was just after my 20th birthday when I scraped a wing tip on my first solo in a Hurricane. For my trouble I was fined 25 piastres (Egyptian currency) and made to clean the Wing Commander's personal silver Spitfire (the pride of Ismailia) on Sunday - a day off for every one else! Later, on my second flight I put up my next 'black mark', this time by running off the end of the runway. The frantic Officer Commanding Flying would gladly have shot me (and all the others) out of hand for breaking his precious Hurricanes. I became extremely familiar with polishing that silver Spitfire!

On completion of my OTU course, it seems incredible that, at 20 years of age and with such little experience, my colleagues and I were now ready to be flung into battle. We were all given a choice of what kind of operational squadron to which we would like to go. My psychological experience back at my Elementary Flying Training School had left me not especially liking aerobatics so I elected for the low-flying rocket-firing squadron in Italy, but this first entailed another course.

Before selection for the Rocket Projectile course, pilots had to be rated 'above average' on the Hurricane because of the skilled nature of the flying needed. It would appear that the Wing Co must have forgotten about my two 'blacks' to recommend me for the course or perhaps he was only too pleased to get rid of me! At No.5 Middle East Training School at Shallufa, just down the road, there were only three Hurricanes, (Mark 4s), with extra armour plating, (to protect the pilots 'Wedding Tackle!'). The Mk 4 was a heavier and therefore slower aeroplane.

Each course consisted of two pilots and lasted three weeks. Each pilot would fire about 75 rockets at tanks and caiques (small boats) and spend the rest of his time learning to fly at 25 feet above the ground! The course was specifically designed to train pilots for the type of operations carried out by No.6 Squadron, based in Italy. It was a dangerous occupation without detailed and meticulous training. To obtain the correct trajectory and accuracy for the rockets in use in those days the aircraft had to be flown very low, straight and level, 25 to 30 feet off the ground and with the gun sight cross set on the target. At 200 or 400 yards the rocket had to be released at 225 mph. If the rockets were released outside these parameters they would either go too high or too low. Better accuracy could be achieved by firing from 200 yards obviously but the aircraft was that much nearer the explosion and flying debris when the rocket hit its target. To avoid this problem a fierce steeply banked turn had to be executed immediately the rocket was released. This manoeuvre, if overdone, could cause what is known as a 'flick stall', which meant that one wing or the other would high speed stall and flick resulting in loss of control very close to the ground. Considerable time had to be spent by the instructors to demonstrate this very dangerous condition in the dual Harvard before the students tried it in the Hurricane. Many times in practice, and particularly on operations, pilots were lost through hitting the ground with their wing tip, high speed stalling or being caught up in the explosion of their own rockets. Flying at such very low levels required tremendous concentration, but it fully prepared the young pilots for the war ahead with the rocket firing squadron.

    On successful completion of the course, I packed my kit once more and set off to join the squadron of my choice - No.6 Squadron somewhere in Italy.

Chapter 3

TO WAR WITH
THE HURRICANE IN ITALY

I left Shallufa on a dirty Egyptian train bound for No.22 Personnel Transit Camp at Almaza near Cairo. On my arrival I was met with many rumours about a barbed wire encampment that had just been built in the camp. It was for the first draft of Women's Auxiliary Air Force to come to the Middle East during the war. Women were a very desirable item to sex-starved males overseas and there was a queue outside the gates at Almaza waiting for the honour of escorting the ladies into Cairo. The girls appeared in their Khaki Drill with long baggy skirts, 'sensible' shoes and lily-white skins. However, as 'Civvies' were not yet permitted overseas, it did not take long for the girls to alter the regulation uniform and make it and themselves more attractive. I was living inside Almaza Personnel Transit Camp so my colleagues and I did not have to queue outside at the gate. I found it most refreshing to be able to talk to an English girl with typical peaches and cream complexion once again!

Within a few days I was on my way to No.6 Squadron 'Somewhere in Italy'. I left Cairo West Airfield in a Curtiss Commando of the United States Army Air Force (USAAF). In a stopover at Tunis the Americans kindly put a jeep at my disposal and I ate well on what seemed to be the standard American diet of steaks and ice cream! As a sergeant I ate in the enlisted men's mess hall (a tent). One thing I found very noticeable, that was different from any

RAF mess apart from the food, was that the Americans wore their hats whilst eating!

Vesuvius had recently erupted and was still smouldering when a very tired Sergeant Pilot eventually slung his kit into a small tent pitched in what had been a football field at the Transit Camp at Portici, Naples. The ground everywhere was covered with a fine grey ash about an inch deep. Life was pretty intolerable for the next few weeks waiting for my onward despatch to my squadron on the other side of Italy. The ash got everywhere, in the hair, the food, shoes, bed, etc and washing facilities were very limited. There was nothing to do all day and life became very boring. Many of the young aircrews found solace in the bottle, consuming the cheap and very poor quality Italian wines available at that time.

On the 20th August with great relief 20 of us packed our ash-ridden bags, climbed into the back of a filthy 3-ton truck and bumped our way down to a Naples goods yard, where we were packed ten to a cattle truck (not long vacated by its original occupants) in horrible smelly conditions. An awful Army Warrant Officer in my wagon attempted to 'interfere' sexually with me as we travelled overnight and at dawn in the morning I was feeling cold, smelly, hungry and very fed up. So I decided to escape the dreadful W/O by jumping out of the wagon when the train next stopped. I did not know where my Squadron was situated as I had been told to report to the regimental transit officer at Foggia for onward transmission. I jumped off and prepared to hitch hike the rest of the way to Foggia. Stiff, tired and loaded down with my kit I staggered out of the goods yard and waited for a lift. Luck was with me as a US Jeep came speeding down the road, with a large black American airman at the wheel, and screeched to a halt. When I explained what I was doing and where I was going and why, the driver gave me a huge grin and said, 'Jump in - there's a 'Limey' outfit with ancient Hurricanes that fire rockets right next to my strip, I'll take you all the way'. The friendly American dropped me right outside the Orderly Room tent at Canne airstrip on the east coast of Italy. It was a lucky lift for me and at long last found me on my wartime Squadron.

The American was from a P51 Mustang squadron on an

adjoining strip. This squadron consisted entirely of elite Black pilots who escorted bombers on long-range missions from Italy. During the early days of WW2 the US would not sanction Blacks flying in the USAAF but later allowed some to be trained as pilots and one or two segregated all-Black squadrons were formed. This particular Mustang squadron, and the others in Northern Europe, went on to destroy more than 100 enemy aircraft between them and won over 150 US Distinguished Flying Crosses between them without losing one single bomber they were escorting. They earned the nickname of 'Red Tails' because they painted the vertical tail fins red. These Black pilots gained huge fame and a reputation as such fearless and efficient escorts that the bomber pilots facing long and dangerous daylight missions from Italy specifically requested them for protection.

The day after I arrived, No.6 Squadron lost a very fine Commanding Officer, Squadron Leader 'Jasper' Brown DFC (Distinguished Flying Cross). On the day he was shot down his promotion to Wing Commander and a DSO (Distinguished Service Order) both came through at the same time. Sadly he never knew about it.

A few days later I climbed into a Hurricane and flew 35 minutes on a sector reconnaissance flight. Later that day I was airborne again, this time in a section of three aircraft bound for Vis, an island in the Adriatic off Yugoslavia. Soon after take-off we were recalled. On landing back at Canne there was a strong crosswind but it was just about within limits for landing. I followed the first two aircraft round to land towards the sea. After touchdown the aircraft ran straight for a time with the tail up, but as my speed slowed and the tail dropped so the aeroplane began to swing off the runway. The only way to counteract a swing was to apply full rudder and brake; this I did but found that I could not prevent my aircraft from gently rolling round in a half circle and plunging nose first into a drainage ditch alongside the runway. I assumed the brakes were weak or spongy and not gripping enough to stop the swing.

However, it was quite by chance over a few beers that evening I heard a rumour that there had been a 180lb tent packed in the fuselage behind the cockpit. I later managed to confirm this but not before I had been blamed for 'pilot error' by my Commanding Officer for not being able to cope with a crosswind landing. I was taken off flying while the hierarchy mulled over what should happen to me. As a result I was sent back to Ismailia for extra crosswind landing training. When I returned I developed a lump in my right groin, which turned out to be a hernia. This kept me off flying for a while. Once my hernia was repaired in the local Military Field Hospital (MFH) in Termoli, I was soon able to get back into action just as the Squadron moved to Zara in Yugoslavia. The war was coming to an end and the Germans were trying to escape from the Istrian Peninsular (including the German hospital ship '*Freiberg*' lying off Brioni). Most of my remaining operational sorties at that time were concerned with action around Trieste to stop the Germans escaping either by land or sea.

One amusing thing the pilots used to do on the way back from their targets to their base, (if they had not fired their wing

No.6 Squadron pilots at Zara, Yugoslavia, April 1945 - self 2nd left, front row

machine guns), was to seek out German camps (e.g. anti-aircraft gun sites or troop domestic sites) mostly amongst the islands in the Adriatic. Because they were tented sites there was no proper sanitation (toilets), so the Germans dug big trenches and put large boards across with holes big enough to sit over. Two or three German soldiers could be sat side by side surrounded by the Hessian sacking, (to give a little privacy); these constructions were known as 'thunder boxes'. As soon as the pilots spotted one of these camps they would swing round and aim their .303 wing guns at the toilets and give a short burst of fire. If any of the soldiers sat on the toilet seats were not actually hit, the frightened men would either jump into the trench and get covered in excreta or else leap out of the Hessian enclosure and leapfrog away with their trousers down round their ankles! I did not have the pleasure of this activity but I was told it was considered to be good fun!

Worthy of mention is one of the last operations undertaken by Hurricanes of No.6 Squadron in WW2 even though I did not take part in it. Four of the Squadron's pilots 'captured' 20 German vessels escaping from Trieste with enemy troops on board. They took off from Pyrkos (Zara) to search for enemy shipping, which had been reported leaving Trieste harbour. The lucky four found 16 ships sailing in convoy away from Trieste. The leader, Pilot Officer Chalky White DFC, led his section in an attack on the front vessel, which quickly hoisted a white flag, so they pulled up, and held their fire. As they peeled away the white flag was lowered so they came round for a more determined attack, and suddenly all the ships hoisted white flags! In the distance, just behind the German hospital ship *Freiberg* which was shadowing the convoy, were four motor torpedo boats speeding to join the convoy and so the same treatment was dished out to them, i.e. dummy attacks, to make them also hoist white flags. With fuel getting short, the Hurricanes had to return to base to refuel and hurry back to their prize. Eventually, however, when they did arrive back the Royal Navy had taken over as the convoy escort, so the disappointed four were forced to return to base.

One of the Warrant Officer pilots who took part in the 'capture' sat in the Sergeants' Mess tent that night clutching a rare can of beer, celebrating, and recounting the tale to me and doubtless embellishing it somewhat! According to him it was called the 'spoils of war' and he would be getting a sum of money as a result of the ship's surrender. The squadron was officially credited with the ship's capture, but no 'salvage' or 'prize' money ever appeared.

When the war in Europe ended on the 8th May 1945, No.6 Squadron was more or less shut down apart from the odd air test. There was much talk of the future and what would happen to the world. To a man, we all marched into the CO and volunteered for service in the Far East.

Fresh supplies of beer miraculously appeared and pilots and ground crews got down to some serious drinking to celebrate the end of the war in Europe. Politics reared its head for the first time and much talk of what the brave new world they had fought for would be like. I was somewhat surprised at the strength of feeling there was for the politics of the Labour Party from most people on the Squadron.

The Yugoslavs around us began to sort out their internal politics too, and relations, always so good between the 'Jugs and the Brits' during the war, began to sour. We pilots began to sense that something was about to happen. And it did with a vengeance!

A restored Hurricane with No.6 Squadron code.

Chapter 4
BACK TO PALESTINE 1945-46

'Move out' was the cry around the airfield at Zara, a week after the war ended. On 15th May 1945, No.6 Squadron was given 24 hours to get out of Yugoslavia all due to the political upset between the new Yugoslav government and the Allies.

The previous evening and night had been terrifying. The Yugoslavs kept firing guns and star shells over and around the camp. The pilots and ground crews began a frenzy of activity in the morning, piling anything that would burn onto a huge bonfire and destroying everything that would not. The enormous bonfire had surplus petrol poured over it and the Discipline Sergeant decided to throw a lighted match on it. The resulting explosion and flash resulted in a much singed and much wiser SNCO! The explosion also frightened the Squadron dog 'Rommel', an Alsatian, who bolted and was never seen again! Everyone also had to say goodbye to poor old 'Donald', the Squadron's pet goose, who would come when called; he patrolled the tents and kept strangers at bay but his great love was to wander around getting drinks from one and all. When he got 'stoned' out of his tiny mind he would take a few steps and fall flat on his face, neck outstretched, a look of utter bliss on his face!

A lot of equipment had to be left behind and some of the Hurricanes that were completely unfit to fly were blown up. Of the rest, those that were only just flyable were jumped into and flown to

November 1945 in Haifa.

Italy. Some pilots flew out Hurricanes to Canne in Italy with no cockpit canopy or the engine cowlings missing and the undercarriages locked down. Things then quietened down for a few days while the Squadron drew breath and gathered itself together.

I nearly 'bought it' after a nice little ferry job taking a Hurricane from Biferno to Brindisi. I was offered a lift back to Biferno in a SAAF Beaufighter and as there was no seat for me I crouched behind the pilot. The flight went well until the port engine caught fire and couldn't be put out. Frankly I was scared as I had no parachute but very fortunately the South African pilot skilfully managed to get things sufficiently under control just in time to get the aircraft down on the nearest airfield before the fire burned through the wing.

On the 30th June 1945 the Squadron was on the move again to Brindisi. We stayed there for a few weeks to have long range fuel tanks fitted then moved out, as a formation of 16 aircraft, on July 28th passing through six countries in four days (via Araxos, Hassani, Maleme, El Adem, Mersah Matruh, Cairo West, and finally Megiddo in Palestine). A Wellington acted as 'Navigator-cum-Shepherd' and the ground crews were in two Dakotas. Only one aircraft dropped out at Mersah Matruh due to a coolant leak. The rest arrived at Megiddo on the 31st July

At El Adem, one of the pilots had one too many beers, tottered out into the sand to 'spend a penny', lay down and passed out and didn't wake up until next morning after the Squadron had departed! His bed had not been slept in, and as he could not be found the spare pilot was alerted and the aircraft all departed without him. The hungover pilot took three days to hitchhike his way all along the North African coast to Egypt and thence to Megiddo in Palestine. He went ballistic when he got back for leaving him behind and it took days before he cooled down!

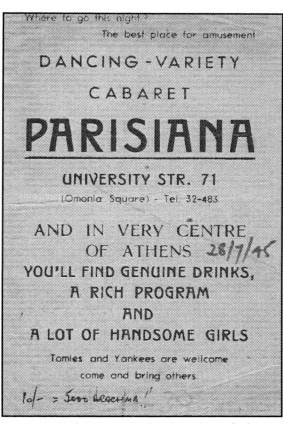

A night out on the 16 aircraft ferry.

The Squadron settled in temporarily at RAF Station Megiddo near Nazereth for a short spell but then moved temporarily to RAF Petah Tiqva before again moving to our permanent base at Ramat David. At Megiddo I got saddled with the job of Sergeants' Mess barman for a month! Our main job at Ramat David became mainly a reconnaissance role searching for illegal immigrant shipping, protecting the Kirkuk-Haifa oil pipeline up to the Palestine border, monitoring the many Palestine Police posts and providing rocket-firing demonstrations for the Overseas Staff College at Haifa and local Army units.

One day in November I was flying low level over inhospitable hills when suddenly my engine lost most of its power. Losing height rapidly I managed to weave through rocky valleys and just made it to a forced landing at Lydda. When the engine was examined six of the twelve cylinders were without ignition. This incident was a sign of the times as all our Hurricanes were now very old and clapped out and this sort of thing was happening more and more frequently.

On 29th November I experienced a tragic and traumatic incident at RAF Petah Tiqva close to Tel Aviv. While attempting to start my engine prior to returning to Ramat David, as I pressed the starter button and booster coil button, a live rocket was discharged from the No.1 rail. This rail had been declared totally unserviceable because the electricians at my base could not induce a current to the 'pig tails' which were plugged into the rocket to electrically fire it. (By some extraordinary and unimaginable coincidence the engine starting system had short circuited to the rocket firing mechanism.) The rocket shot between two hangars and landed in a nearby settlement killing

November 1945 - Ramat David.

No.6 Squadron Hurricane at Ramat David in Palestine, with my fitter 'Tich' Brook

an 84-year old man, injuring two others and killing a lot of turkeys. The incident arose because another Hurricane had made a forced landing at Petah Tiqva due to a failing engine and had eight live HE (High Explosive) rockets on board. The armament staff at RAF Petah Tiqva had never seen or dealt with rockets before and due to the terrorist situation they declined to keep them overnight. They pleaded with me to take them away on my aircraft and despite the fact that I knew I could not jettison the rocket from my No.1 rail, (I would have to bail-out if my engine had failed) I agreed to do what they so desperately wanted. As a result the normal safety procedures were ignored and I personally plugged in the pigtails before start-up, whereas they should have been plugged in at the end of the runway immediately before take-off. However, as the armourers there did not know how to do this, there was no alternative - with devastating results!

This all happened at the height of the troubles in Palestine. I was disarmed of my revolver (carried by all pilots at the time) by the Station Commander and driven round to the blitzed Kibbutz to apologize to the bereaved and injured. It was a very traumatic and alarming moment that I have never been able to erase from my memory - apologising to grieving old ladies and a newly widowed one. The smell of cordite was still in the air, dead turkeys everywhere and ambulance crews tending the wounded. But worst of all angry armed Israeli's pointing guns at me! I had an awful feeling I would be shot at any moment!

The whole incident had made headlines in the *'Palestine Post'* newspaper so when I returned to Ramat David I found my bed had been moved out of the room I shared with another pilot and no one else would now share a room with me! My NCO pilot colleagues visualised terrorists making an assassination attempt on me, or a bomb being thrown into my hut! It was really a bit of tongue in cheek black humour but it made its point! In fact, though, a similar thing happened shortly afterwards. A 213 Squadron pilot intercepted an illegal immigrant ship and the Irgun terrorists had somehow mysteriously found out who it was, put a black-bordered notice in the *'Palestine Post'* to the effect that he would be assassinated! He was posted away from Palestine in a hurry!

After a lengthy investigation an obscure electrical fault was found in the rocket firing and engine starting systems of my aircraft at Petah Tiqva, which was traced back to modifications not carried out at Farnborough in 1942! A Court Martial exonerated me due to the extenuating circumstances and considered my actions were excusable. Had I been found guilty, I would undoubtedly have been given a 96-day spell in a military prison!

Shortly after I was promoted to Warrant Officer and thereby hangs a tale. There was a strange ritual in the Sergeants' Mess whereby Flight Sergeants, newly promoted to Warrant Officer, had to pass a little 'test' before they were allowed to join the 'elite' band of Warrant Officers who usually sat together. A row of different brands of whisky was lined up in glasses on the bar and the 'new boy' (me!) was blindfolded and had to sip each one and nominate the brand (i.e. Bells, Famous Grouse, and Glenmorangie etc.) If successful he was welcomed into their midst - if not, he had to go away and practice till he got it right! Luckily I got it right first time!

I flew a Spitfire (a Mk9) for the first time when the Squadron received four Spitfires to replace some of its ageing Hurricanes. However, on the day the new Spitfires arrived at Ramat David we all turned out to witness the event, but one landed with a tail wheel problem, pranged and was written off! All the 'old soldier' pilots who were 'boat happy' and waiting for their postings (repatriation to the UK at the end of their overseas tours) were aghast and gazed in sheer horror. They immediately declared they were definitely not going to risk their necks in one of those new fangled powerful death traps if that was how difficult they were to land! Nevertheless, as a

March 1946 - a spot of leave in Beirut - with 'Nobby' Clark.

young 'keen' member of the Squadron, I volunteered to fly them and had no problem. Going off in the Spitfire was one of the most enjoyable experiences I have ever had. I still say to this day that the Spitfire was the nicest, most manoeuvrable and beautiful aeroplane I have ever flown (and I have flown over 60 different types!)

My time in Palestine and on No.6 Squadron came to its inevitable end and after a round of various farewell parties I departed by train to Egypt and No.21 PTC to await my departure back to the UK after nearly three and a half years overseas. I left for the United Kingdom on the 18th May via 'MEDLOC', a mixture of ship, rail and road, (ship to Toulon, train and road to the UK).

Once back in the UK I began to think about whether to get 'demobbed' and what to do as a civilian. There was little prospect of getting into civil flying in those days and going back to an office job was not an option I could face. So I began to think seriously about staying in the RAF. My next posting to fly Meteors made my mind up and I 'signed on' for an initial three years. Little did I dream then that I would still be flying in the RAF at 65 years of age!

April 1946 - the lovely Spitfire on No.6 Squadron.

Chapter 5
THE EARLY JETS 1946-48

After some well-earned leave, and as a newly promoted Warrant Officer, I was posted to No.56 Squadron at RAF Bentwaters near Ipswich on the 9th July 1946.

It was by way of a feather in my cap that I, a mere NCO pilot, was posted to one of the very few squadrons flying the most modern jet of the time, the Meteor Mk.3. Nowadays the Meteor seems very slow in comparison to modern aircraft, but in those days it was one of the fastest planes in the air.

RAF Bentwaters was an old wartime airfield of tin huts with German POWs still employed around the domestic site. It was an idyllic environment; the taxyways meandered through woods and dispersed hutted sites and there was only the one resident squadron with full station support. I noted, as I rode my bicycle along, that the station was liberally sprinkled with WAAFs and they all appeared to be slender and beautiful. (Well, they would, wouldn't they - I had just been three and a half years overseas!) The sight of these delightful girls lifted my spirits even higher. I also found the Sergeants' Mess to be very homely and friendly. I was a very happy and contented young man!

When I arrived at the door of my allocated accommodation I was greeted by three redundant Polish aircrew who had various jobs such as Station Warrant Officer, NCO i/c Messes and Motor

Transport drivers etc. These three were industriously engaged every night (and for most of the day I suspected) in making Perspex ornaments and trinkets for ladies to wear. The work used to go on late into the night and the grinding, drilling and polishing kept me awake until the early hours. In the mornings when I awoke my hair was covered in fine Perspex dust! I felt obliged to move out as soon as possible and let the Poles continue their trade alone.

I was given a couple of dual rides in the squadron 'Hack', an old Oxford, the only aircraft available to teach twin-engine flying. I had never flown a twin-engined aeroplane before and so asymmetric flight, i.e. flying a twin-engined aircraft with one of its engines shut down, was a mystery to me. It should be remembered that there were no dual control jets in existence at this time and no official course to attend. One just read the Pilot's Notes, received a quick verbal briefing and got on with it.

The jet is such a beautiful smooth and completely vibrationless machine after a piston-engine plane that I felt that I was gliding out of the dispersal in a Rolls Royce car. My moment to take-off had come, strapped in the Meteor with the engines giving an unfamiliar whine as I turned onto the 6000 feet long runway (as it was then),

No.56 Squadron, Bentwaters 1946.

having done every check at least twice! It was wonderful to sit in a nose-wheel aircraft for the very first time and be able to see where I was going. But even more wonderful was the feel of the two Derwent engines giving full power. In the air the smoothness and lack of noise in the cockpit was something I find difficult to describe. The climb was meteoric (no pun intended), after the Hurricane and Spitfire, and effortless up to 20,000 feet in a clear blue sky. It gave me one of the most joyous feelings of my life. A few aerobatics over East Anglia and then I flew back to Bentwaters to land. Suddenly it was all over and it had seemed so easy.

The Meteor was an extraordinarily kind and undemanding aircraft to fly and land, but always provided one did not approach too fast. The engines were so reliable that there was hardly ever an engine failure. As part of my training on the new type however, I had to shut down one engine and carry out a single engine landing for practice (which was, in effect, not a practice but the real thing!) on only my third flight in a Meteor!

It was a glorious summer that year with many warm balmy evenings spent pedalling to the nearest pub that had any beer. The beer shortage that summer in 1946 meant that accurate research had to be done in the Sergeants' Mess to find out which brewery delivered to which pub and on what day. Our WAAF girl friends were as charming as they were attractive and we, the only three NCO pilots on the Squadron, used to cycle out with them each evening to the pub that had had its weekly delivery of beer! The WAAFs on the station were MT drivers; parachute packers, engine fitters, instrument repairers etc. and all of them seemed happy, well-balanced girls like the pilots they went out with. They had responsible jobs by day but liked to relax in the evenings. These were happy days for all of us.

All good things must come to an end and 56 Squadron moved to RAF Boxted, just outside Colchester, but sadly the girls had to remain at Bentwaters. We three NCOs moved into a Nissan hut and lived in somewhat primitive conditions. The only good thing about Boxted was that there was a pub just across the road from our tiny hut. A small hole, just big enough for us to slip through soon appeared in the fence and we almost became permanent residents of the pub! There were the odd hilarious evenings in Colchester, one in particular, when some of the officers were arrested by the police for relieving themselves on Woolworth's window in Colchester High Street! Officers and gentlemen!

The rugby season was approaching and it so happened that the AOC (Air Officer Commanding) 11 Group wanted a particular rugby-playing pilot from 12 Group to strengthen his 11 Group's team. After much 'wheeling and dealing', I, despite my protests, was selected to be the pilot exchanged for the rugby star. With sorrow I bade farewell to 56 Squadron.

I unpacked my bags at Horsham-St-Faith near Norwich to join 245 Squadron in 12 Group. My arrival coincided with the Squadron leaving for Lubeck, North West Germany, for an Armament Practice Camp. The next six weeks were great fun, shooting at air and ground targets with live ammunition and flying low level sweeps over West Germany. The evenings were enjoyable, spending the time meeting the frauleins and drinking the German beer. On one occasion two frauleins actually fought each other for the favours of one NCO pilot but he didn't like either of them, which made it a very amusing evening!

Back at Horsham St. Faith, 245 Squadron was equipped as what was known as a 'Cadre' establishment, i.e. it was at half strength. As with most small units or groups, we were a most happy

Inspection line-up of Meteor 3s at Horsham St. Faith. I am far right.

No.245 Squadron pilots, Horsham St. Faith, 1947 - self at rear left.

band of three NCO pilots and five officers flying eight Meteors as part of the defence of Britain from the possible Soviet threat - i.e. the Cold War.

The winter of 1947 was truly cold and dreadful. RAF Horsham St. Faith had to shut down due to lack of coal and most non-essential personnel were sent home (except me and the Sick Quarters staff!). There was no hot water and no central heating with temperatures well below freezing. I had picked up scabies from a dirty blanket at RAF Tangmere and, after all but essential people had left, I was confined to Station Sick Quarters for treatment. That consisted of being immersed in a bath of some sort of solution three times a day, which was OK with warm water, but when all the heating went off I had to have my baths in a freezing cold solution! It was bloody awful!

Occasionally the Squadron was asked, as part of Public Relations, to give demonstrations for the Press and it was on one such occasion that I had a very narrow escape. I was No.3 in a formation doing low-level passes for photographers on the airfield. On

NCO pilots of Horsham St Faith Wing.

one pass I went into line astern behind and below the No.2 but when the leader went really low it meant I was almost scraping the ground. Every movement is exaggerated slightly by each aircraft in a formation. So when the No.2 moved up and down in his efforts to keep station with his leader, my movements followed likewise, but I was afraid to drop down too far in case I struck the ground. Each pilot's eyes are glued to the aircraft in front and not watching the proximity of the ground. So, in my efforts not to go too low the inevitable happened - I caught the No.2's slipstream and went out of control. It was a miracle that my aircraft jerked upwards and not down or I would have been killed instantly. I managed to recover, calmed my fright and rejoined the formation to complete the sortie for the Press.

July and August 1947 were spent at Lubeck again for an Armament Practice Camp. Not long after we arrived a most incredible thing happened. A Royal Navy squadron (perhaps it would be kinder not to name it) also came to do an Armament Practice Camp. They came in two waves of eight Seafires (naval version of the Spitfire). They had all been briefed that there were two parallel runways, but one was under construction and littered with road rollers and contractor's plant, piles of sand and cement etc. The other runway was made of pierced steel plate or metal planks. They were late in arriving and it was almost dark but despite all the warnings they had about the two runways (neither had night flying lights) they insisted on doing a typical navy deck landing approach on the wrong runway! Their normal method of approach to a ship involved a tail down straight-in approach (to catch the deck hook) so the pilots could not see forward over the big Seafire nose. The normal approach RAF Spitfire pilots used comprised a curving approach so that the runway was always in view. Just like lemmings all but two or three of the 16 Seafires landed one after another on the wrong runway despite frantic warnings from Air Traffic. I and all the other RAF pilots just gazed in disbelief at the carnage.

The Meteor wing at Horsham-St-Faith consisted of four squadrons i.e. Nos.74, 245, 257, and 263 and these Squadrons provided a fair number of NCO pilots in the Sergeants' Mess. They were all single and lived in the Mess so it was a very lively and happy place. The girls of Norwich seemed a gorgeous lot and a few eventually married some of the pilots. The 'Sampson and Hercules' dance hall was a popular Saturday nightspot where many a girl friend was met, courted, jilted or eventually married. The Norwich pubs were

Outside the Sergeants' Mess, RAF Horsham St Faith.

1st April 1948 - Captain Al Tucker USAF with fellow members of No.245 Squadron.

very popular and many of the landlords became good friends of the young jet pilots who were fit and smart. We were fond of telling tales and downing pints of 'Black and Tans' (Stout and Mild) at eleven pence ha'penny each, (in today's money - just below 5p!). Another popular spot was a dance hall in Sprowston where a very young Geoff Love played his trombone. His playing was so good all the dancing would stop and we would crowd round him with popular applause.

    About this time the Horsham Wing began converting to the much more powerful and faster Meteor Mk4 and the RAF and the USAF (United States Air Force) started to exchange pilots. The first USAF officer to come over joined 245 Squadron. He was a tall and very charming man by the name of Captain Al Tucker who was obviously handpicked. He was a superb pilot and an able administrator and soon joined the 245 Squadron aerobatic team. One thing about him has always remained etched in my memory - one day during a Press visit when Al was asked what he thought of the new Meteor Mk4, his laconic American drawled reply was, 'She climbs like a homesick angel'! The Press had a real ball with that! This latest

Meteor was, at that time, faster than anything Al Tucker had flown with the USAF and he was certainly impressed!

At this time there was a very nice looking young WAAF employed on 245 Squadron whose duties should have been merely involved in servicing the aircraft's instruments. Her name was Teddy Rowley and although it was not part of her duties around the aircraft, on each flight she consistently climbed up the side of the Meteor to assist with strapping me into my cockpit and, after hovering around, unstrapped me on my return! (I was very flattered by this!) The Flight Sergeant i/c the ground crews knew what was going on and turned a good-humoured blind eye. Her efforts paid off as we started going out together and a romance developed which would probably have ended up in marriage had I not been posted to the OCU at RAF Bentwaters as an instructor.

One day in December, I was airborne when the weather clamped down over Norwich with little warning and our Meteors could not scurry back in time despite an urgent recall. Homing devices were a bit primitive in those days and GCA (radar letdown called Ground Control Approach) did not exist at Horsham-St-Faith, so it was 'every man for himself' once we got below cloud. The cloud was right down almost touching the top of Norwich Cathedral spire and rain lowered the visibility so much that we had great difficulty finding the runway and with our fuel so low it meant we could not divert to another airfield with better weather. However I, and the other three aircraft with me, just managed to land safely with almost empty fuel tanks. It turned out to be a happy ending with personal congratulations from the C-in-C Fighter Command, who just happened to be in Air Traffic Control on a visit and witnessed the whole thing!

A few days later, in similar weather, the same thing happened but this time ended in disaster. One of the three Meteors managed to land on the runway but the other two were completely out of fuel and crashed. One went through a farm building hitting a threshing machine and slid through a barn. It showed how strongly built the Meteor was that the pilot could step out shaken but unhurt. The third pilot was also fortunately unhurt after skidding across roads and fields. The leader's engines died while he was taxiing back to dispersal! We young pilots were always forced to watch our fuel states like hawks, particularly in the unpredictable East Anglia weather, because we only carried about 40 minutes fuel for each sortie. Such was the state of our fighter aircraft defences to defend the UK in the Cold War of that time.

All good things must come to an end and my tour as a fighter pilot was nearing its completion. Having spent over two years flying Meteors it was time for me to teach others and pass on my experience. Hence on the 27th January 1948 I was flown to 226 OCU (Operational Conversion Unit) at RAF Bentwaters in the Station's old Oxford. I bade a fond farewell to little Teddy Rowley and we determined to keep in touch but the exigencies of the Service being what they are we slowly drifted apart.

Chapter 6
OCU INSTRUCTOR - 1948

After Horsham St Faith it was back to delightful Bentwaters but unfortunately all the WAAFs had departed. It had become No.226 OCU where pilots were taken direct from Training Schools to be taught the current Fighter Command fighter tactics and to be converted to the current fighter aircraft in use. The pilots who were to fly twin-engined types were given dual instruction in (really unsuitable) aircraft like the Oxford. Single-engine students were checked out in

No.226 OCU Oxford model.

No.226 OCU Tempest model.

the Harvard. The fighter aircraft in the front line at that time were the Gloster Meteor 3s being superseded by the vastly more powerful Meteor 4, the twin-engined de Havilland Hornet, and the single-engined de Havilland Vampire and Hawker Tempest.

The RAF had changed its rank structure for NCO aircrew and now I was Pilot II Rose N.E. The ranks were graded from IV to I, and finally 'Master Pilot' (which is the only aircrew rank remaining today from this system and is the equivalent of Warrant Officer.) This awful new ranking only lasted a couple of years and it was eventually thrown out as unworkable.

No.226 OCU Meteor model.

My job was responsible and quite demanding for one so young and relatively inexperienced. I was given the Meteor 'side of house' and so, without the background of a formal instructors course, I set about teaching young men (not much younger than me) the rudiments of asymmetric flight. It was a case of showing them what I could in the Oxford, then teach them as much as possible about the Meteor and send them off solo. (I well remembered my own first Meteor flight and the apprehension I felt). Next I would lead them about the sky in various formations, teaching them tactical formation, close formation and dog fighting.

As time went by I became involved in the Meteor 4 project and the Vampire part of the OCU. I went off for the first time in a Vampire but I was not too impressed. My biggest impression, apart from the 'lack of poke', was that maybe I had forgotten to lower my undercarriage and my bottom was going to scrape along the runway as I landed! (The Vampire was set very low with the belly nearly touching the ground).

The OCU was a big one. It had many aircraft of differing types and the number of students passing through was considerable,

No.226 OCU Hornet at Bentwaters with self in cockpit.

even though in 1948 the RAF was less than one third of its wartime strength; yet it still possessed a large number of fighter squadrons, albeit most at half strength.

As I blossomed as an instructor I also became embroiled in the Hornet/Tempest flight and was soon flying these two aircraft as well. Neither of them had dual versions so it was a case of Pilot's Notes in one hand and throttles in the other! The Hornet was very nice to fly in comparison to the Tempest, which had a nasty habit of swinging on take-off owing to its massive power and propeller torque reaction. Soon I was also doing conversions to type and teaching the art of tactical flying to Tempest and Hornet students.

I would often fly Mr Bill Waterton, the famous Gloster Javelin test pilot, to and fro between Bentwaters and Staverton in an Oxford as part of my duties. Bill Waterton visited the OCU to lecture to the Meteor 4 students and to pass on his experience. I got the distinct impression Bill wasn't too impressed with my low-level split-arsed dash beneath the low clouds through the hills to get into Staverton airfield (Gloucester) when the weather was bad.

In June 1948, as a welcome break from the tedium of OCU instructional duties, I was offered a 20-day detachment to Olympia in London to join three other pilots to stand in front of the actual Meteor on display that had recently broken the world air speed record. I was sent in the capacity of a Meteor 4 pilot, because at this

At The Olympia, London, June 1948.

time these pilots were the 'elite' of Fighter Command. It was a pleasant three weeks for me, busy and proudly answering the multitude of questions from the public who flocked in their thousands to Olympia's Royal Tournament.

The RAF was settling back into a peacetime routine with the Central Flying School starting to flex its muscles once again. The staff visited 226 OCU to check the ability of the instructors and to find out if all the instruction was standardised. I was checked by a CFS examiner who was horrified to find that I was not a qualified flying instructor trained at the 'Holy of Holy's', the flying instructor's college at RAF Little Rissington. As a result of that visit, within a few months I was on my way again, this time to the Central Flying School.

Chapter 7
CFS AND 6 FTS - 1948-50

On the 21st July 1948 I reported to the Central Flying School at Royal Air Force Little Rissington to become a Qualified Flying Instructor on No.106 Course. It was a six-month exacting and detailed course but it taught students how to analyse their own flying as well as how to teach others to fly. One aspect of the course I found difficult to get to grips with was operating the Harvard from the back seat on the final approach. I could not see forward over the front pilot and the big nose of the aircraft, and my short stature made it difficult to lean over and peer out of the side of the cockpit on landing.

During the last month of the course the students progressed to what was called the 'type flying' phase. The idea was to allow the ex-bomber pilots to fly fighter types of aircraft and vice-versa so that, when they were instructing at a Flying Training School, they could answer questions from their pupils about what flying the various types was like. Having flown fighters so far in my career, that part was 'old hat' to me, but what I really wanted and had set my heart on, was to fly the Lancaster and the Mosquito. As a general rule no one on the course went solo in the Lancaster but I cajoled and badgered the Lancaster instructor and, with the help of a good word from my own instructor, Lt. Ray Lygo RN, my wish was granted. A special case was made for me (the young, keen NCO!) and so I did

Lancaster model.

the usual initial dual in the Lancaster (this really whetted my appetite), followed by two more comprehensive dual flights before being launched solo as the captain. The flight engineer detailed to fly with me was askance at this and took a dim view of risking his life with such an inexperienced young pilot on type. However, we managed a safe hour and I apparently handled the aircraft and landings well enough to placate him. He earned a couple of beers off me that evening in the Mess bar!

Ray Lygo then taught me to fly the Mosquito and I found it a beautiful aeroplane to handle. Ray went on to become the Captain of the famous aircraft carrier HMS Ark Royal and eventually a very senior Admiral in the Royal Navy.

The days at Central Flying School were happy ones for us students and most rewarding. We rose early, worked hard, flew hard, and swotted hard, then for a little relaxation we went down to the pub in nearby Bourton-on-the-Water. I have an enduring memory of that pub - most evenings a young lady would come in and order a pint of

Mosquito model.

beer, then pick it up in her teeth and down it in one go! Astonishing but true!

Little Rissington was a thriving and well-disciplined station; the SNCOs on the course were all experienced pilots and lived in a homely Sergeants' Mess. The officers lived in the huge Officers' Mess but in the evenings we all mixed together in the local pubs and at the weekends most of us trooped off to Cheltenham.

Many of the officers on the course went on to become senior officers and one or two even rose to Air Rank. Most of the NCO pilots were later commissioned and also went on to higher rank. It has always been recognised by aviators that CFS produced some of the finest and most professional flying instructors anywhere in the world. Later in our careers this qualification helped us attain promotion and superior flying appointments. For example, I subsequently had some very interesting and rewarding flying jobs purely and simply because I became a Qualified Flying Instructor. At one stage, without that qualification, I would undoubtedly have been grounded at a time when there were too many pilots chasing too few jobs.

At the end of the CFS Course I was posted to No.6 FTS (Flying Training School) Ternhill near Market Drayton, which had Tiger Moths and Harvards, but the Prentice was soon to supersede the old trusty Tiger Moth.

I was eagerly looking forward to getting a 'lump of flesh and bone' and moulding it into a pilot. I remembered my own early days as a student pilot and made sure I taught my students with patience

Prentice model.

Avro Lincoln model.

and understanding. I always made sure they were never terrified like I had been when I was hanging out of that cockpit upside down over Rhodesia!

A succession of students went through my hands in the Harvard, and it was always a proud moment for me as I watched them step up to receive their 'Wings'. It reminded me of my own 'Wings' parade as if it was only yesterday.

About this time a gorgeous WRAF Sergeant was posted into Ternhill. Her name was Dorothy Maybury and she caused quite a stir in the Sergeants' Mess! Subsequently she was to play a very big part in my life as my wife.

There were some welcome breaks from the flying training routine such as my visit to RAF Binbrook to fly in a Lincoln. The object was to expand my knowledge and background of Bomber Command so that I could talk to my students about it. For two nights I flew on 'Exercise Foil' which entailed flying in the black of night at 20,000 feet over London and Birkenhead Docks. I was cold and scared and peered out at dark shapes beside, under and above, all flying in the same direction. It made me realise what those heroic wartime bomber crews had to contend with, including flak, night fighters and bad weather. Occasionally there was bumping and jolting as we ran into the slipstream of other aircraft, not surprising considering there were hundreds of aircraft in the bomber stream. The idea of the exercise was to test the UK Air Defence System at night and give bomber crews mass attack experience. Later on, during a similar exercise in September, two Lincolns collided in mid-air and both crashed in flames killing both crews. I made a mental note that that kind of flying in bombers was not for me in peacetime (or any other time, come to that!) and I felt I couldn't recommend it as a career to any of my students!

In 1949, No.203 AFS (Advanced Flying School) was set up at RAF Driffield, Yorkshire. It was the first of its kind to cater for jet dual instruction. The two-seat, dual-control Meteor Mk7 was just off the production line. So no longer was the inexperienced young Meteor pilot strapped into a jet to take-off without dual instruction first, which I had to do three years earlier. To staff the new AFS the RAF cast around for QFIs with previous jet experience, which is why I was sought after and posted to Driffield while only half way through my basic instructional tour at RAF Ternhill. I have to say I was not all that keen at that stage of the game as it meant a separation from my fiancé.

After a few hours flying in the back seat of the Meteor Mk7 with an instructor, I went off for a solo sortie in a Meteor Mk4 and thereby hangs a tale! Bear in mind that I had quite considerable experience on Meteors, including the Mk4. Normally the aircraft accelerates quite rapidly and the elevators become effective with the increasing airflow. At about 90 knots the nose wheel should rise gently in response to backward pressure on the control column so that the aircraft can be 'flown off' the runway at about 110 knots. On this occasion I was fast approaching 110 knots with the nose wheel still firmly in contact with the runway. Not knowing what was wrong and

Model of the Meteor 7.

fearing some elevator problems I abandoned the take-off and the aircraft careered through the fence at the end of the runway ending up virtually undamaged in a very wet and muddy field. The intrepid and shocked aviator (me!) clambered out, squelched my way round the aircraft and had a good look at the elevators and the trim wheel in the cockpit but could not see anything amiss. The crash tender appeared in minutes and gave me a lift back to my Squadron. My Squadron Commander seemed satisfied with my explanation but 20 minutes later the Wing Commander Flying appeared, incandescent and his face red with rage. He glared at me, with filthy shoes, muddy wet trousers, hair unkempt and screamed at me, 'Your flying is reflected in the way you dress, get off my station!' A nice polite officer!

The trouble was that life had not been too sweet for this Wing Commander recently because there had been a series of accidents involving Meteors at Driffield and the Air Ministry was on his back as a result. Most of the accidents were caused through practising single-engine approaches with one engine flamed out i.e. stopped, but this meant that it was never really a 'practice'; it was the REAL thing. As a consequence, the inexperience of the young pilots resulted in an average of about one accident per week. Most of these were through getting too low on the approach, opening up the throttle to full power on the live engine and losing rudder control, (instead of reducing the power to regain control) and crashing. (The inept practice of flaming out the engine was stopped eventually and the exercise was done with the engine throttled back i.e. idling). The high accident rate was reflecting adversely on the leadership at Driffield and this particular crash was the last straw for the long suffering Wing Commander, and particularly so as I was a potential instructor in this case!

I downheartedly packed my bags as instructed and departed back to RAF Ternhill before the Wing Commander could heap any more abuse on me. However, being back with my fiancé helped to soften the blow! I went back to my old job on Harvards for a short time but then was sent to fill a vacancy on the Prentice flight.

Soon after I arrived back I received a personal letter of apology from the Air Officer Commanding 23 Group about my treatment at Driffield, which also explained that the aircraft was a known rogue with a high-unstick speed and I should have been briefed on this unusual and misleading fault. My pride was satisfied but I still felt grieved that I could not have remained instructing on Meteors. However, as it turned out I would never have attained the superb posting and job, which came my way at the end of my renewed tour at Ternhill.

On the Prentice flight life was never dull. One day I was doing a favour to a fellow instructor by dropping him off at RAF Finningley, near Doncaster, whilst carrying out a cross-country (navigation exercise) with one of my students. The rather large fellow-instructor and his kit was squeezed into the back seat of the Prentice and all went well until the engine stopped for some unaccountable reason over the Yorkshire hills and dales about four miles west of Sheffield. The selection of a suitable forced landing area was extremely difficult in the somewhat inhospitable terrain. However, I spotted a postage stamp size piece of green within gliding range, which turned out to be a football pitch and I managed to get the Prentice down in one piece on it. The student and I had a rough ride back to Ternhill in the back of a 3-ton truck and the aircraft followed later on a 'low loader'.

The Prentice was a bit slow and underpowered and I found performing aerobatics in it was like trying to loop a double-decker bus! Nevertheless, as my fiancée Dorothy was a Sergeant in the WRAF, I was able to fly her quite frequently and she loved aerobatics! On April 8th 1950 we married and we started 'living out' in Market Drayton.

At one point a Balliol was sent to Ternhill for the instructors to 'play with' and give their opinions as to its usefulness as a replacement for the Harvard. We had great fun with it converting one another. It was powerful and nice to fly and had the feel of the Spitfire - but it never really caught on as a dual basic trainer.

On the 30th June I was involved in a horrific accident in a Prentice. I was instructing and demonstrating to my student the art of making a forced landing in a field after engine failure. For this practice the engine was throttled back to simulate the failure and a likely field was chosen to which to glide down. As the engine was 'cut' high up the fine detail of the fields could not be accurately assessed

My wedding day to Dorothy - 8th April 1950.

and structures such as high-tension wires were not readily apparent.

Things were going well until we turned on to the final approach to our selected field. Since the ground sloped upwards towards a dark green belt of trees ahead of us on the horizon it made it very difficult to spot the poles behind trees, and the high-tension (HT) cables stretched across our approach path. It was too late when we did spot them against the dark background.

Despite applying full power and pulling the aircraft up, the wheels of the Prentice (which did not retract) struck the top HT cable and snapped it. There was an enormous lightning-like flash with a lot of sparks. The cable whip-lashed and wrapped itself around the undercarriage, gripping it firmly and bringing the Prentice almost to a halt in mid-air. The aircraft then dropped like a stone amid sparks and flashes; the fixed undercarriage was driven into the ground right up to the under-surface of the wings! In the event the sturdy Prentice did not burn and neither of us was hurt. The local fire brigade arrived but were not called into action. A large part of Shropshire was blacked out for 40 hours with no electricity! Whether this accident put my student off flying I never did find out but the lad did not complete his course.

In early October, those in authority who 'post' people in the RAF showed what appalling dimwits they could be. A posting had arrived for me to report to RAF Calshot, near Southampton, to instruct on Sunderland flying boats. I had never flown a flying boat, had no maritime experience and the only experience I had on four-engined aircraft was the little I had at CFS. Furthermore, captains of flying boats, (indeed all four-engined aircraft), had to be of officer rank. It was blatantly obvious to everyone but the authorities at the Ministry of Defence that the posting was a monumental mistake - as it certainly proved to be. I went to see my Wing Commander Flying and he agreed. Within a few days he sent for me to tell me my posting was cancelled! It seemed that the 'desk warriors' in authority thought that any qualified flying instructor could instruct on any aircraft after ten flying hours on the type! They did not learn by this mistake because six weeks later I was posted to instruct on the Hastings at the Long-Range Transport Operational Conversion Unit at Dishforth, Yorkshire. I marched in to see my Wing Commander again but this time the posting staffs were not going to retreat. Once again, after much discussion it was obvious that a NCO with very little four-engine experience and no transport aircraft operations experience could not go and instruct at a Transport OCU. But evidently, to save face, this time I was made to go!

Model of a Balliol of No.6 FTS.

I packed my bags and travelled north to RAF Dishforth. On the way I decided that attack was going to be my best policy. Soon after arriving I screwed up all my courage and entered the office of the Wing Commander Flying with my logbook under my arm. The intrepid Pilot II (me with that awful new rank!) explained how I had been messed about and I was absolutely fed up with the way I had been treated when it was blatantly obvious that both postings were inept, and, if I was refused a job at Dishforth I would take out a 'Redress of Grievance' (A 'Redress of Grievance' is a lawful military procedure for obtaining justice and is not to be taken lightly by anyone.)

This attacking posture obviously had the right effect and in no time I was offered a very attractive job as an instructor on the Overseas Ferry Unit in glorious Devon!

Chapter 8

THE FERRY TRAINING UNIT 1950 - 1952

On the 15th November 1950, I reported to No.1 (Overseas) Ferry Unit at RAF Chivenor, Devon as a Qualified Flying Instructor on the Ferry Training Unit. This turned out to be one of my more enjoyable flying tours - part instructing and part ferrying.

No.1 Overseas Ferry Unit was responsible for collecting new RAF aircraft from the factories or storage units and delivering them to wherever they were needed throughout the world, and then bringing back the old 'clapped-out bangers' to the UK. Apart from the small training and conversion flight the main body of the Ferry Unit consisted of about 20 officer aircrew and about 50 NCO pilots, navigators and signallers. RAF Chivenor was an extremely nice place to be based, with Barnstaple, Ilfracombe and Bideford nearby. Those who were married lived out around the base in very pleasant accommodation. Dorothy, pregnant with our daughter to be, and I lived in a small flat in nearby Braunton.

Firstly some words about the daily life on the Ferry Unit itself and its aircrews. Quite a large part of the pilots' lives was spent living out of a suitcase somewhere along the network of routes to various parts of the world. Sometimes this could be a tedious business as space in a military aircraft, especially jet fighters, was at a premium, so most pilots had to have two or three soft bags instead, which could be squeezed into ammunition bays, or any small space about the aeroplane. Carrying enough clothes to transit from freezing Europe to tropical Singapore was a real problem. Nevertheless, because it was such an enjoyable job, flying so many different types of aircraft and seeing the world at the same time, morale was always at its highest.

The aircrews were a very amiable and happy band who, despite living in one another's pockets most of the year round, got on well together, both on the route and back home at Chivenor. Away from their base, along the routes, the ferry crews had to live in sweaty uncomfortable accommodation, eat greasy food and fly without complaining whilst suffering stomach upsets and local conditions that were, at times, too hot and at other times too cold.

In those days the RAF airfields along the routes all had 'Transit Messes' and no matter what time of the day or night of landing or take-off the meal was always the same - a greasy egg, tomato, sausage, beans, and even greasier chips. As if that was not bad enough the beer was nearly always warm and the beds, sometimes bug-ridden, were in uncomfortable, hot, cramped, shared rooms (no air-conditioning in those days.)

The single-seat aircraft would normally go as formations of three or four so that if one of them experienced engine failure or had an emergency, with the pilot having to bale out over the sea or mountains, the others could pin-point the position and radio for help. Sometimes the formations spent long hours hanging on to the leader's wing tip in lumpy clouds. This demanded the utmost concentration and would often be followed by a hazardous letdown to an unfamiliar airfield in poor visibility through tropical rain or sandstorms. Anyone who was not up to such a demanding job did not last long on the Overseas Ferry Unit!

There were few flying jobs at that time in the RAF that demanded so much professionalism and common sense. Rapid changes of sleep patterns, climate and cooking called for cast iron constitutions and superb fitness and, despite living out of a suitcase for as much as two weeks at a time, they always somehow contrived to look presentable in the evenings.

Where there was no technical assistance, the pilots refuelled and serviced their own aircraft, often in very remote locations, and even in some cases carried out minor repairs. There were times when there was no spare part available so the pilot, and the rest of his formation, were stuck with their aircraft until it arrived; often this meant being away a month or more. Considering that when they left home they took clothes for about a week, they could arrive back in the UK smelling a bit high! Despite these many privations, the overseas Ferry Unit never failed to deliver the goods wherever and whenever it was needed.

No.1 (O) Ferry Unit and the Ferry Training Unit moved from Chivenor to Abingdon near Oxford early in 1951. Although my main job on the Training Unit was to convert the ferry pilots to new types of aircraft, a very large part of my responsibilities was to teach the pilots to be able to contend with all in-flight aspects of loss of an engine on multi-engine types. No simulators were available to demonstrate that sort of thing in those days.

I felt it a privilege and honour to have come to a unit such as this to teach these stalwarts, particularly as a humble NCO. The Ferry Training Unit had never had a NCO instructor before and I was initially viewed with a modicum of suspicion as a sort of 'spy in the sky' that might tell 'tales' to the hierarchy! However, eventually they came to trust me and I became 'one of them'.

In June 1951 a very unfortunate incident occurred. I had been converting an officer pilot to the Mosquito. He had completed all the asymmetric power exercises without any problems and was at the stage where he was competent to practise single-engine flying safely on his own. I spent an hour and forty minutes with him practising single-engine approaches and overshoots until I was absolutely sure he could do them solo then sent him off to practise them. It was my contention that by carrying out these manoeuvres solo, in ideal training conditions, pilots would gain confidence and know they could cope, if it happened to them in an emergency.

The pilot completed a couple of landings and an overshoot on one engine, but the next time he came round on one engine he got too low and slow, opened up the power to try to stretch his approach but lost rudder control and crashed just short of the Abingdon runway. The pilot was killed outright and I felt really awful - I had never had a student crash before, let alone kill himself.

The Mosquito had this undeserved bad name for its single-engine performance but it was rarely the aeroplane at fault - mostly the pilot. After this accident I found some of the pilots were even more nervous of the Mosquito. Many ex-wartime pilots, for example, were hide-bound with the idea that they should never 'turn towards the dead engine' in the circuit. So I started to institute demonstrations at a safe height to show what a safe aeroplane the Mosquito actually was on one engine. I did this partly by carrying out slow rolls with one engine feathered and rolling into the dead engine. It simply terrified some of the pilots. One of them got out after a dual sortie and refused to fly with me in a Mosquito again!

Perhaps the most hazardous flying conversions were to the Beaufighter, which had no dual control version. I was frankly nervous as all I could do was stand behind the pilot where I could not reach the controls and talk him through the many manoeuvres needed to enable him to go off solo. Teaching asymmetric overshoots and landings was a nightmare! Fortunately the vast majority of the ferry pilots were of a very high standard of competence - nor did an accident ever happen to a Beaufighter. The Brigand and Meteor were fine as there were dual control versions in the Buckmaster and Meteor Mk 7.

The Buckmaster.

Model of the Brigand.

On one occasion, while collecting a Mosquito from Hawarden Maintenance (or Storage) Unit, I ended up climbing out of the wreckage on the airfield! I had lost all my brake pressure in the air during a shakedown flight and I made an approach to Hawarden's (Chester) longest runway. The windsock (well away from the runway) indicated the runway to be almost into wind but unfortunately I had not taken into account the deflection of the wind by the huge de Havilland factory hangar half way down the runway. After a good solid wheel landing with the tail well up, everything seemed to be under control, but as soon as the tail wheel touched the runway the aircraft started to weather cock to the left into the wind which was blowing round the big hangar. The Mosquito became uncontrollable without brakes and started to career off the runway. I hurriedly switched off the fuel and magneto switches and prayed. The right undercarriage leg collapsed and the aircraft ended up in an undignified smoking heap but did not burn. Fortunately unhurt, I leapt out unable to believe my luck in surviving without a scratch.

On another occasion I was allowed a ferry during a lull in the FTU training schedule to deliver a Meteor Mk10 to Kabrit and bring back a clapped out old Mosquito Mk34. One of the worst features of the Mk34 was its safety speed of 175 knots (the speed at which it is possible to control the aircraft at full power in the event of a sudden engine failure), especially in the very high temperatures of the Canal Zone. I took off with my navigator, and came unstuck from the runway at about 80 or 90 knots and we stared at the airspeed indicator, for what seemed an eternity, as we very slowly accelerated over the Bitter Lake in the Canal Zone till it reached 175 knots. We were just heaving a sigh of relief when smoke started to pour out from behind the instrument panel. There was a smell of burning rubber and all things electrical went wrong as well. I turned quickly and shot straight onto the Fayid runway (even though it wasn't the one in use!) and as we ran along the runway my 'brave' navigator jettisoned the canopy and leapt out long before I stopped!. Just another case of an old 'banger' that should have been scrapped where it stood instead of having it flown back to the UK only to be scrapped there!

The CO of No.1 (O) FU was being taught to fly the Valetta by one of the two Ferry Training Unit officer instructors who only had B1 categories. Only an instructor of A2 category was permitted to send another pilot solo so, as I was an A2, I was asked to give the Wing Commander a final check immediately prior to his going solo. I spent over an hour with him before I felt confident enough to send him off on his own. Unfortunately as he came in for one of his landings he bounced too high, failed to take the correct action, i.e. open up and go round again, and ended up crashing the Valetta on the runway! This was the second time I had a pilot crashing after sending him solo. No one was hurt except the Wing Commander's pride.

The Yugoslavs bought a large consignment old Mosquito Mk38s and I scrounged a couple of days off in between instructing and delivered one of the first ones to Balajnica (Belgrade) via Frankfurt and Zagreb. We went as a loose formation of eight aircraft with a Valetta shepherd to bring the crews home. Before we left, the Ferry Unit CO gave us a very stern lecture about the dangers of over imbibing the local Slivovitch and forbade us to drink the stuff! (he had done a proving flight previously and learned the hard way!). When we arrived we were given a VIP welcome in a hangar, plied with copious quantities of the dreaded Slivovitch, taken to a hotel and told not to leave it. To compensate for that everything was on the 'house'. Well. what did you expect! We all had the most horrendous and painful hangovers and in the Valetta on the way home some of us were quite ill! The CO was not best pleased with me and I received a monumental 'bollocking' for allowing it to happen because I was an 'Instructor' on the unit and should have set an example with better leadership! Some hope, knowing me!

In September my CO noticed I was losing weight and was becoming a little withdrawn and remarked upon it. For example, quite apart from my normal conversion and check flying, over the past two years my log book showed 230 sorties of hazardous instruction in asymmetric overshoots and landings in Mosquitos, Valettas and Beaufighters etc.

I was, frankly, feeling ready for a rest so I applied for a transfer out to pure ferrying. My CO agreed to rest me from instructing and recommended my transfer. He told me, before I left, that he had forwarded a recommendation for the award of the Air Force Medal (AFM) as a thankyou for my work on the Training Unit. However, he told me later that it had been turned down at Command level because it was felt I should shoulder some of the blame for the Mosquito and Valetta crashes! Some you win and some you lose but I felt it was a little unfair to blame me for someone else's mistakes.

During my time as an instructor on the Ferry Training Unit, my daughter Linda was born at Princess Mary's Hospital, RAF Halton on 8th August 1951. Now as 1953 dawned my son Christopher was on the way - to be born on 8th June 1953, also at Halton.

In those days Married Quarters were hard to come by - if one had not served long enough in the RAF and/or had only been married for a few years - or did not have several children. In those instances, there was not much chance of a Married Quarter under the RAF's 'points' system.

When I moved to RAF Abingdon, my wife Dorothy and I had to be separated initially because we did not have enough of those 'points'. So we scraped together enough money to buy a 22-foot caravan and lived in a nearby farmer's field. We were woken each morning by a herd of cows rocking the caravan by rubbing themselves against the side - a very rustic life! Eventually we were able to move on to the RAF caravan site and lived close to the end of one of the runways with our baby daughter Linda.

At that time we had a cocker spaniel called Samba who would sit happily outside the caravan on nice sunny days guarding his little sister in her pram. On most days the postman just walked past the pram and Samba remained friendly but on one occasion he stopped and peered in at little Linda, so Samba leapt into action doing his 'guarding thing' and bit the poor postman! I used to take him to work occasionally and Samba consistently barked at navigators and signallers if any of them came anywhere near the pilots' crew room! Presumably he was able to recognise the half wing brevets they wore on their uniforms!

It was not until my son, Christopher, was born that we gained enough 'points' to obtain a rather primitive Married Quarter at RAF Benson. In the Quarter all we had to cook on was an old black coal burning range, which also boiled the kettle and heated the lounge and domestic hot water through a back boiler. This was also the only heating for the whole house.

Nowadays of course, things are much better for all Servicemen and their families. It speaks well for the loyalty of the Air Force wives in those days that not many faltered despite the extreme privations which they suffered. But those wives implored their not-too-well-off husbands to buy small electric 'Baby Belling' cookers to do away with the drudgery of cooking on the coal ranges; so many of us splashed out bought them. Consequently the power lines to the married quarters at Benson became red hot with overloading and caused many blackouts and great pandemonium in 'Works and Bricks' (Air Ministry Works Dept.) circles.

So ended my time with the Ferry Training Unit and I moved across to the Overseas Ferry Unit.

Chapter 9

THE OVERSEAS FERRY UNIT
1952 - 1954

The next two years, after my transfer from the Ferry Training Unit, were very busy and entailed a great deal of time away from home. It was hard for the young wives who were left at home alone with very young children and especially those who could not drive and lived in remote areas. In those days few, if any, of the NCOs could afford cars and buses were few and far between. A marriage had to be strong to weather the problems brought on by constant and indeterminate separations. My marriage was no exception and the strain showed.

In 1952, the RAF had nearly 7000 operational aircraft flying worldwide (today the figure is more likely a hundredth of that). There were 21 squadrons in Germany, 20 in the Middle East, 13 in the Far East and some more units in Malta, Gibraltar, Kenya, Southern Rhodesia and Cyprus. So the Overseas Ferry Unit was kept at full stretch supplying them all with aircraft and flying the old ones back. Quite often without instructors to give dual flying on any of the types they had not flown before, (for example, return ferries), the pilots were forced to simply read the Pilot's Notes, climb in and 'get on with it'. Despite that, accidents were very few and far between entirely due to the very high level of flying experience of the ferry pilots.

Because I had the necessary experience on the types

Dakota model.

involved, I was allotted many of the 'one off' tasks. Some of these involved the older and more 'clapped out' aircraft that were scattered around the world. Some should have been burned on the spot rather than ferried home as most of them were only fit for a museum,

On one ferry I flew an old Dakota back to the UK via an island called Car Nicobar in the Indian Ocean. The very small island is about one third of the way between Malaya and Ceylon (Sri Lanka) and was manned by 'one man and a dog' i.e. a Sergeant, an airman and one or two locals. It was basically there as a refuelling stop for the FEAF Valettas going to and fro to Negombo in Ceylon. My enforced nightstop there was an awful experience sleeping in the aircraft! By the time I got back to UK I had flown 92 hours in 16 days and I was shattered! The Dakota was a slow old bird,

Car Nicobar with Dakota KN467, 2nd July 1952 - the Staff!

Hornet Mk3 model.

which was only capable of cruising at about 130mph.

1953 dawned cold and snowing as I departed to Singapore to deliver a Hornet. The Hornet was probably the fastest piston-engined fighter ever to see service with any of the world's air forces. It was a single-seater so we ferried in pairs to enable us to 'shepherd' each other in case of emergencies or loss of radio. We carried long-range fuel tanks under each wing, which gave us very long range without refuelling. Each leg was in the order of 1500 miles at altitudes of 18-22,000 feet (breathing oxygen). We depended on map reading, which often was not possible because much of the time we were above cloud, so we flew as accurately as possible to our pre-computed flight plans and when in radio range of airfields, on our route, we called for check bearings or for homings to our destinations. Once clear of Europe and the Mediterranean, ground aids became rather sparse and often badly manned which meant we were very much on our own, apart from the ADF we carried. Weather also became a problem as often we were flying through or round large cumulus clouds in the tropics with no weather radar.

Of course, there were compensations like, for example, while waiting for a flight back to the UK, relaxing in the sun beside the swimming pool at Changi! However, the return flights were often a horrible opposite! We departed from Changi in the back of a Hastings of Transport Command for a five-day grind back to RAF Lyneham. The Hastings took about eight or nine hours flying each day to flog its way to England with overnight stops at Negombo, Mauripur, Habbaniya (Iraq) and Idris. That was the only type of flying involved that we ferry crews really hated. It was downright uncomfortable, cold and boring and, to add insult to injury, really grotty night stop accommodation. Having said that, if we got lucky, some return flights were in civil airliners sitting in luxury and quaffing as much free alcohol as we could drink served by dolly bird hostesses!

Although not from my log book, there is an amusing story from the historical record of the Ferry Unit about a Master Pilot, a phlegmatic, unflappable and very able pilot who was ferrying a Meteor Mk7 to Singapore. In the rear seat was a navigator and on the way from India over Burma they encountered very severe weather and became separated from the other aircraft. In trying to avoid the storms, (the cockpit of the Meteor 7 is unpressurised which meant they could not fly above the storms), they got well off track and were lost. Their compass had malfunctioned after being struck by lightning and they were fast running out of fuel. They spotted what they thought was a level green field and decided to do a wheels up landing on it before they ran out of fuel and the engines failed. Unfortunately, the field turned out to be a rice paddy field with a foot of mud and water beneath the green surface.

When the aircraft came to rest and they realised they were uninjured, they decided to sit and have a nerve-calming cigarette before pondering their next move. At this point some natives appeared from the surrounding jungle, so help was at hand - or so they thought! The next second the pilot heard a loud hiss and a plopping sound and on turning round saw the navigator sitting in his inflated dinghy amongst the rice shoots. Their rescuers, (anti-government Burmese rebels), thought this was hilarious and pointed their rifles at the pilot indicating that he should follow suit, which he did with all haste. It was not very funny when they realised that their rescuers were, in fact quite hostile. The two of them were taken prisoner. During the night, in the jungle, the navigator started snoring. When the pilot's shouting did not stop him, the guard cocked his rifle and was about to shoot him! The pilot managed to wake the navigator in the nick of time!

These Karen rebels thought they were delivering the Meteor to the Burmese Government, with whom they were at war.

The Karens were actually pro-British and when the two finally convinced them they were taking the Meteor to Singapore, they were escorted to Rangoon. Just before they were released on the outskirts of the city, the rebels advised them to have a shower as quick as they could because they were about to blow up the Rangoon Waterworks! They had just had their shower and were drying themselves when there was a loud explosion and the water went off! Their troubles were not completely over yet - they now had to convince the Burmese authorities that they were not delivering the aircraft to the rebels! Once they had achieved this they were soon on their way home.

No one back at the Ferry Unit in the UK knew what had happened to them so they were posted as 'missing presumed killed'! Not exactly the sort of thing that happens in peacetime to a non-combatant outfit!

Five days after I returned from a Singapore ferry, the River Thames was running very high and Canvey Island was threatened with flooding. The Government declared a state of emergency. I was despatched, in a Valetta, to run a shuttle between Zurich (Switzerland) and Manston in Kent with a load of 4500 lbs of empty sandbags every trip. The task was aptly codenamed 'Operation Canute'! Returning on one occasion to Manston, my No.2 (right) engine failed after leaving Switzerland. After some thought, I decided to carry on to Manston to ensure the sandbags got through and to make it easier for the ground crews to repair the Valetta. Not perhaps a 'good' decision but I thought I was doing the right thing at the time.

Next I was off in another Hornet Mk3 to Singapore. On the leg from Bahrain to Mauripur things started to go wrong with the cooling systems on both my engines; the starboard engine coolant temperature went above its permitted maximum even though the radiator shutter was wide open, which meant that the coolant was leaking. This left me no alternative but to stop the engine and feather the propeller.

Under normal conditions this would not be a problem as the

Hornet could fly quite well on one engine and would have made it to Mauripur easily. But then I found that the radiator shutter on my good engine was stuck in the one-third open position and would not open further! Since I was flying on one engine I needed more power from the remaining engine and so, it too started to overheat. That area of the world was most inhospitable and I started to worry about the sort of reception I would get if I had to forced land in the desert. I had my 'Ghoolie' chit, which offered a large reward if the pilot was handed over 'intact' and I fervently hoped the bloodthirsty local Arabs could read! I put out a 'Mayday' call and received a reply directing me to the RAF base at Sharjah about 80 miles away. I just made it before the engine boiled over! My aircraft was repaired after five days and my No.2 and I left for Mauripur and on to Singapore. Returning to UK we had no luck in getting a civil flight so we were subjected once more to the usual five-day grind in the noisy, cold and uncomfortable Hastings.

There are not many people in any walk of life who can truthfully say, 'There but for the grace of God go I.' but this was so in my case. I was converting to the new Canberra jet bomber at Benson with another pilot. On the day I was to have gone solo in it my colleague asked me to change places, as he wanted to take his wife to hospital. I willingly did so, but tragedy struck and my friend crashed and was killed on the sortie I should have flown. At that time, the Canberra was having teething troubles with tailplane trimming. The trimmer was operated electrically and the whole tailplane angle was altered to obtain the desired trim. To trim the aircraft in the pitching plane (fore and aft) the pilot 'blipped' a trimming switch, which was spring-loaded to return it to the neutral position when released. The problem was in the electrical system, which could experience a short circuit causing the trim to run to full nose down,

Brigand.

which the pilot was unable to over-ride by pulling back on the control column, even with all his strength. Consequently the aircraft would go into an uncontrollable nose dive. This was what happened, and but for the swapping of flights I would have undoubtedly been killed instead. Subsequent to this accident, Canberras were modified with a 'fail-safe' system whereby the pilot had to activate two switches at once. However, no further Ferry Unit conversions to the Canberra were attempted for a while

I had a rather amusing incident after ferrying a Brigand to Kabrit in the Suez Canal Zone, with a navigator and a signaller. We were then to go on as passengers to the Far East and bring back an old Dakota to the UK. While we were waiting for the usual scheduled Hastings flight to the Far East, the C-in-C FEAF's (Far East Air Force) brand new VIP Hastings, complete with VIP crew, came through Fayid and the captain offered us a lift to Changi. The three of us leapt at the chance as this Hastings offered total comfort. The VIP fit included large and very comfortable seats, wall mounted fans

The C-in-C FEAF's gleaming Hastings.

and, best of all, decent food served by a nice-looking WRAF Air Quartermaster!

The VIP crew were immaculate whereas, we, the intrepid Brigand crew were in filthy crumpled standard blue-grey flying overalls. When the VIP Hastings touched down at RAF Changi there was a reception committee of Far East Air Force Air Commodores and Group Captains, headed by the Officer Commanding Flying. They were waiting at the bottom of the steps, all eager to meet the C-in-C's new pilot and inspect his brand new aeroplane. Since my crew and I were the only passengers on board the Hastings, we went straight to the rear door and climbed down the steps. The reception committee paled under their Singapore tans to see three very scruffy NCOs when they were expecting very smart officers to fly the C-in-C. They did not realise that these 'scruffs' were not the C-in-C's crew. I did not realise the unintended deception until the Wing Commander rather sheepishly started to introduce us as the C-in-C's crew to the assembled hierarchy! The Wing Commander's face was a study when, seconds later, the resplendent Hastings captain and his very immaculate crew in their smart white flying suits appeared in the aircraft doorway. We 'Scruffs' were sent packing to the Sergeants' Mess where we entertained the guffawing SNCOs with the story. Presumably the 'Top Brass' also saw the funny side afterwards?

Two days later though, we had our own equally high-powered committee of Senior Officers to see us off, as we departed in Dakota KN 497. There were many sad faces as it was the last Dakota in the Far East Air Force. The trusty old 'Daks' had all been replaced with Valettas. The date was 1st July 1952.

Later that July, I set out from the UK to deliver a Valetta to the MU at Seletar, Singapore. In the back was an Auster for the Army Air Corps in Malaya. In July, in southern Asia, the South West monsoon is at its peak making flying a very rough experience especially down India's west coast. We encountered the monsoon just south of Karachi and remained in it at 9,500 feet all the way to Bombay. In an aircraft like the Valetta there was no radar. So once we were in cloud we could not pick our way around the cumulonimbus clouds, with associated violent up and down draughts, hail and lightning, contained within it Lightning struck the aircraft at one point but the bonding and earthing system was good and the strike did no damage. We were strapped in tight and the signaller was forward in the co-pilot's seat helping me maintain control while the navigator tried desperately to keep his air-plot and log going. The Auster creaked and groaned in the back and we began to worry whether it might break loose. After an hour and a half our problems worsened when we heard that Santa Cruz (Bombay) was experiencing severe thunderstorms and heavy rain, reducing visibility to a quarter of a mile.

There was no suitable alternative airfield within range so we struggled with the letdown procedure with hail bashing against the aircraft and great rumbles of thunder and lightning flashing all around us. We managed to catch a glimpse of the runway through the threshing windscreen wipers in the tropical downpour and were greatly relieved to put the aircraft down on a runway that was more like a lake. The rest of the flight was uneventful - this time we sat back in comfort in a BOAC Argonaut to fly home to the UK, very relieved it wasn't in the dreaded Hastings!

There were very few four-engined aircraft squadrons permanently stationed overseas and so we didn't have much business ferrying for them. However, a few days later I went across to 23 MU at Aldergrove with a flight engineer to collect one. While we were air testing and 'shaking down' a Mark 2, the automatic pilot mechanism caught fire. The cockpit filled with smoke and the flight engineer disappeared to deal with the fire. With just the two of us on board I could do nothing but sit and wait. The flight engineer put the fire out but in so doing he burned his right hand. After the Aldergrove Medical Officer had bandaged him up he complained bitterly that the worst feature of the affair was that he might have difficulty holding a pint of beer in the Sergeants' Mess that night! We were less than impressed at having to sleep in some awful old wartime huts in freezing temperatures, with coke fires that went out half way through the night, and ablutions 100 yards away! The locals aptly named them the 'Arab Quarters'! The aircraft was changed and we returned to Benson and ferried it out to Malta.

After we handed it over at Malta, we were to ferry back an old Lancaster Mk3 (SW287). My flight engineer and I went over to the squadron and had a good look over it. It looked a real old 'banger' and thoroughly 'clapped out', (but well, was not the 'Lanc' a trusty old bird or so my flight engineer convinced me!). We found a multitude of things we thought ought to receive attention before we ferried it and made our feelings known to the Flight Sergeant in charge. In turn he passed it on to the squadron's Commanding Officer. Next day the two of us were summoned to the Wing Commander's office to be 'torn off a strip' - the Wing Commander's vehement view, which he forcefully expounded, was - 'If the aircraft was good enough for his crews then it was good enough for *prima donna* ferry crews!' As mere lowly Flight Sergeants we felt disinclined to argue with an angry Wing Commander!

Next day we climbed on board and took off. First of all the wheels would not retract and only after a Herculean struggle by the sweating and cursing flight engineer did he eventually get them up. We cleared with Luqa Air Traffic Control, and the signaller was soon busy getting in contact with Malta on W/T. Then suddenly he chirped up that he was getting sparking with his W/T equipment and every time the VHF (radio) button was pressed up front there were sparks and shorting noises coming from the radio equipment box near him.

While this conversation was going on, the No.1 (left outer) engine failed! The flight engineer went into frenzied overdrive and the engine was quickly shut down and feathered. During our return to Malta, while the flight engineer was trying to establish the cause of the engine failure, the signaller's voice came over the intercom with a note of anxiety to the effect that he was being asphyxiated with petrol fumes. The now frantic flight engineer shot back to see what the problem was and came back white-faced to say that it was not good news! There was a serious petrol leak in the crossfeed line and it was pouring into the bomb bay. I immediately told the signaller to shut down all his radio equipment and the crew was forbidden to use any electrics since the slightest spark might ignite the petrol vapour. We communicated with each other by shouting. Because the radios were all shutdown we could not declare our

The Anson I left behind at Berka Two.

emergency to Air Traffic Control.

More problems were to come - there was only one suitable runway available and nowhere to divert. This runway had a strong crosswind, which unfortunately was blowing from the wrong side (the left) for our three-engine landing. If the aircraft swung into the crosswind from the left, it would normally require full right braking and if the brakes were weak it would need power from the port (left) outer engine to help stop the swing - but it was feathered!

I frankly admit I was very worried. With great relief we got our undercarriage green lights. We turned onto the final approach and flew past ATC waggling our wings to try

Anson model.

79

to let them know we were in trouble. Air Traffic Control must have realised there was an emergency and fired off a green Very to indicate it was clear for us to land.

As we touched down on the main wheels and the speed started to decay the inevitable happened the moment the tail came down. The Lancaster started to swing into the wind - the wheel brakes were not strong enough and would not hold the swing, but with excellent and intelligent crew co-operation my flight engineer helped pull off the landing. I had both hands on the control column and (with my short legs) full right rudder applied while my flight engineer, without being told but with superbly astute action, gave a long blast of full throttle to the No.2 (left inner) engine and together we managed to keep the Lancaster straight. We switched everything off in dispersal and sat sick with reaction and the smell of fuel, which was cascading from the closed bomb bay doors and pouring all over the dispersal. Undoubtedly, but for my flight engineer with his vast wartime Lancaster experience, plus his timely co-operation, we could very easily have swung off the runway, crashed and gone up in flames. His reaction over a wind-down beer in the Luqa Transit Mess was, quote, 'It was a bloody sight safer over Germany in the war than flying with you!' unquote! (I didn't like to tell him I only had about 15 hours experience on Lancasters!) The Malta Squadron's CO was extremely sheepish!

The next incident highlights the fiasco of bringing old and useless aeroplanes back to the UK. With another pilot, a navigator and a signaller, we flew down to Kumalo in Southern Rhodesia to pick up two old Ansons and ferry them to the UK. The idea was that one Anson carried a navigator and the other a signaller and as a team we would operate together. Most of the flight planned route was over the most inhospitable terrain one can imagine landing at such little known places to refuel as - Lusaka, Ndola, Kasama, Tabora, Entebbe, Juba, Malakal, Khartoum, Wadi-Halfa and then back on the 'bus route' via the Canal Zone to the UK.

While we were flying across Lake Victoria into Entebbe, I had one of those 'green apple quickstep' problems. It was a common occurrence in the tropics due to food hygiene, at a lot of the stopover places, being practically non-existent. It was a case of 'get to the little can' (called an Elsan) stowed in the back or have an accident in the seat! I made my signaller leave his seat by the W/T equipment and sit in the pilot's seat because this Anson had only one control column on the pilot's side. The poor protesting man was entrenched in the seat and told to keep the wings level and under no circumstances lose sight of the other Anson (because the navigator was in the other one!) He was taken aback with my yelling at him with such insistence but he manfully gave it a go. His complaint was that he was 'a bloody signaller and didn't know how to fly aeroplanes!'

All went well for a short while, but my rushing down to the rear of the cabin and squatting on the little 'can', caused the trim of the aircraft to alter. My weight at the rear made it tail heavy and so the aircraft began to climb. Sat there, sweating profusely, I could feel the nose-up change of attitude and the decrease in noise as the airspeed fell off. I realized what was happening, but I could not get off the pot! Meanwhile up front the signaller was rigid with concentration trying to keep the wings level but he had no idea that he was allowing the aircraft to climb and it would stall. With superhuman effort I managed to heave myself up the fuselage, with my flying overalls down around my ankles, to find the signaller gripping the control column so hard that his knuckles were white, sweat pouring from his brow, eyes glazed and staring straight ahead. I grabbed the control column and pushed it forward to stop the impending stall and then realised to my horror that the other Anson was nowhere to be seen! There was nothing I could do but to eventually pull my overalls back up and get back into my seat and sort things out. I got a rough course to steer for Entebbe from the navigator in the other aircraft over the radio after explaining my predicament. Both Ansons eventually spotted each other again when the lakeshore jungle appeared on the horizon approaching Entebbe.

We four intrepid aviators staggered on in our two tired old Ansons until we landed at Benina in North Africa. Here the other Anson became so unserviceable it appeared doubtful if it would go any further, so I pressed on alone and, of course, the inevitable happened. About one hour along the track to Castel Benito out of sight of land, the left engine began to bang and clatter and eventually seized up. I turned round to return to Benina with full power applied to the remaining engine to reduce the unavoidable height loss - Ansons did not normally have enough power to maintain height in hot climates on one engine. This particular Anson was very battered and was a bit of a lash-up of bits from other marks of Anson which meant it was experiencing even more drag than usual, so it was impossible to maintain height on one engine, even down at sea level! I just managed to reach the coast, still losing height, and was down to about 200 feet when I luckily spotted a small strip of sand in the desert, which was an old disused wartime airstrip called Berka II. I was able to slap the wheels down just before touchdown, which saved the aircraft from unwanted damage and possible injury to us.

Soon after landing we were amazed to see a jeep appear over the horizon in a cloud of dust, carrying some USAF (United States Air Force) airmen. The kindly Americans whisked us away back over the horizon to a small batch of tents beside a little radar station and fed us with huge steaks and ice cream, all washed down with ice-cold beer. Later that day a 3-ton truck arrived from RAF Benina with a guard for the Anson to relieve the Americans. We bumped our dusty way back to Benina in it.

A 'Green Endorsement' in my flying logbook came my way for that little incident and, later that month, I was promoted to Master Pilot. Not long after that I was posted to the Officer Cadet Training Unit to be commissioned as a Pilot Officer. Things moved rapidly.

Chapter 10

OCTU & THE FAR EAST - JET CONVERSIONS 1954 - 1957

I packed my bags at No.12 Spitfire Square to go to the Officer Cadet Training Unit at RAF Jurby on the Isle of Man. In its very inflexible way, the RAF insisted that my family vacated our Married Quarter immediately because I was posted away from RAF Benson and would not be returning there. It was RAF policy that you did not return to the same unit or station as an officer, having been an 'other rank' there. (I often wondered what happened if you failed the OCTU and were returned to your unit?) Families of servicemen had to tolerate far more home disturbance than the public at large could ever conceive. In fact, in my RAF career my family were uprooted and had to move home 26 times from 1950 (when I married) to 1979.

While I was at OCTU, my wife and two small children were obliged to go and live with relatives until it was known where I would be posted after the course - it does not make for a settled mind on a demanding course.

I found the 12-week course physically and mentally exacting. The cadets with me were mostly mature aircrew of 30 odd years of age. We had to rise at 6am to frantically 'bull' (clean and polish) the hut we lived in before breakfast for a daily inspection. We were not allowed to wear the new anodised buttons (God knows why, since all the rest of the Air Force wore them) so we had to clean our buttons every morning, press our clothes and maintain a shine on our boots good enough to shave in! Each day was spent alternating between 'square bashing' (drilling), lectures, physical training and playing at 'soldiers' with the RAF Regiment. The 'Educators' (Education Officers) had a great deal of influence with regard to the course content; thus a lot of the time was spent writing essays, learning 'Chairmanship' and lecturing for five minutes on a simple object, (a match stick or a pin). Most of us 'old soldiers', (i.e. NCO aircrews), found this type of activity a 'pain in the backside' to put it mildly!

The big 'joke' was that because we were serving aircrew, MOD had a 'box' of 'OQs' (Officer Qualities) stored away for each of us, to be distributed at the review board at end of the course. This, we joked, would ensure we were not 'scrubbed' for 'lack of education' and/or 'lack of OQs' at the end of the course, so we didn't have to worry about trying too hard! A Master Pilot had been personally recommended by Air Marshal Sir Hugh Pugh Lloyd for a commission, (he was his personal pilot) but the OCTU failed him for lack of OQs! The s...t hit the fan when the AM found out - his view was that if he said he had the necessary OQs, then it was only necessary for the OCTU to indoctrinate him on deportment and duties of an officer! Quite right too I say. Some of the OCTU staff were posted and generally pilloried! Well done that Air Marshal! The Master Pilot later received his commission back dated to the end of the course

The great day dawned when we donned our brand new officers' uniforms and became a bit embarrassed at first when airmen saluted us. The big disappointment at the end of the course, when the postings were read out, was that most of us were given non-flying jobs! I was extremely disenchanted to find I was posted to RAF Middle Wallop to be trained as a Fighter Controller!

I was re-united with my wife and family and we moved into a rented, old thatched cottage in a tiny village called Little London near Andover, while I was on the two-month course. The village was really quaint with one pub, no shops and just two buses a day into Andover. I used to catch the 8am service in the morning. Each passenger was so well known to the driver that if anyone didn't turn up he would hold the bus, while someone dashed off to collect him, and waited till he arrived!

At the end of the course, I decided to volunteer to go to the Far East where there was a vacancy on a Fighter Control Unit at Changi in Singapore. I felt I had to make the best of a bad thing and there might be some compensation for being taken off flying by taking my wife and children to Singapore - a superb posting for most. (I was familiar with RAF Changi from my flights there on the Overseas Ferry Unit).

I was sent off on leave to await 'joining' instructions. The RAF had left my family and me homeless without a parent unit so we were now obliged to go and lodge in my mother-in-law's small house in Manchester. It was very cramped for us all and not at all ideal.

Incredible as it may seem, I could still have been waiting there until this day! I waited and waited. After eight weeks I rang the Air Ministry several times but no one knew anything about 'Pilot Officer Rose' - my name and posting had been completely lost! It was not until three months later I eventually left the UK for the Far East leaving my family to travel out on their own by sea in a troopship to join me in Singapore!

I had been an NCO pilot for 12 years and had become accustomed to life in the Sergeants' Mess. Now I was a brand new Pilot Officer and I felt a bit apprehensive about life in the Officers' Mess. I had the theory pushed down my throat at the OCTU about being an 'Officer and a Gentleman', what to wear, how to behave etc.

I scrubbed off the grime of five days travel cooped up in the back of a Hastings and unpacked my kit in the spacious airy rooms of RAF Changi's Temple Hill Officers' Mess. Rather nervously I descended the stone stairs to have a beer before my evening meal and as I reached the long stone flagged corridor to the bar the sound of loud and raucous singing reached my ears. The sight that greeted me as I entered the bar through the slatted swing doors has always stuck in my memory!

The large ceiling mounted fans were entwined with toilet paper, the ends of which were flicking round on the wet floor. The floor of the bar was awash with spilled Tiger beer (the local draught) and in the middle of it all was a group of about 30 drunken aircrew still in flying kit shouting and singing, each one clutching a pint glass. Some Distinguished Flying Crosses, for operations against the Communist Terrorists in the Malayan jungles, had just been announced that morning and the recipients had been celebrating since lunchtime!

I was invited to join the party and immediately felt a bit more at home! However, it crossed my mind that this sort of behaviour would not have been tolerated in the Sergeants' Messes I had lived in previously!

Next day I went across to the Southern Sector Operations Centre over on the far side of the Changi runway and booked in. It was a Ground Control Interception Centre (GCI) and kept watch over the sky approaches to the Malay Peninsular with big rotating radars.

The building was air-conditioned and was pleasant and cool compared to the sticky 85°F outside. The air conditioning was not installed for the comfort of the operators; it was necessary for the efficient operation of the radar but it was quite pleasant working inside. However, I hated the job of peering into radar screens, in the gloom, so it was not long before I went over to the FEAF Communications Squadron and made myself known. I was soon keeping my hand in flying on the other side of the airfield in my spare time.

Three days after I arrived the monsoon struck. For three days and nights it rained so heavily that it was almost impossible to drive across the airfield. Water swept off the Officers' Mess first floor concrete overhang in a solid sheet and anyone who attempted to pass through it to the entrance was almost drowned. The floors inside the Mess were wet with condensation and clothing became saturated. The bed sheets were so damp that you could almost ring water out of them. Although the temperature was 80 to 90°, the wetness and wind seemed to chill the air and made it feel cold. There was no point in going out anywhere so the Officers' Mess bar did a roaring trade!

After the third day the torrential rain eased off, but it continued to rain on and off. The monsoon drains overflowed and the reddish muddy water swirled around everywhere. At last the sun poked through again and life gradually returned to normal. I ventured out to the Changi Officers' Club - a beautiful spot with a swimming pool, bar, restaurant and a battery of 'fruit machines' which devoured my 20-cent pieces! I was beginning to realise that RAF Changi was undoubtedly an excellent place to be stationed. I was well paid and the climate was not all that bad, just a little sticky at times. The resident families all seemed happy and contented with their lot. My family was sailing out by troopship from the UK via the Suez Canal (just before it was closed by the Egyptians) and would arrive sometime in January. Life looked as though it was going to be very pleasant indeed.

When my family arrived, we moved into a little bungalow in

Changi Officers' Club pools.

Siglap on the East Coast Road about five miles from RAF Changi. It was not very sumptuous but adequate enough for a short time. As 1955 advanced and my name reached the top of the waiting list, I was fortunate to move my family into a superb brand new two-storied married quarter on the domestic site. This move caused raised eyebrows about the allocation and jealous remarks were overheard among Group Captains and Wing Commanders who were living in the less sumptuous, old bungalows. They could not understand how a mere 'sprog' Pilot Officer was allowed such superior large accommodation over more senior officers! But the officer who ran the Quarters' list was a strict, honest 'by the book' character who wouldn't be influenced. As a name came to the top of the waiting list, the next Quarter was allocated. It was the luck of the draw but it didn't go down too well with some of the more senior officers' wives!

No. 155 Lloyd Leas was designed for hot weather and gracious living. It had green marble floors and staircase and open plan rooms. The Amah (nursemaid, cook and cleaner) lived in her own accommodation out at the back and a Keboon (gardener) looked after the ample garden, and best of all the RAF paid for it all!

At that time the war in Malaya was at its height and it was getting harder for the Army to catch the terrorists in their hideouts in the jungle, so the RAF was constantly looking for new ways to bomb them. It was a bombshell therefore, for me to be detached to a strange job to become very closely involved with the war on the Communist Terrorists. My terms of reference were to ' find a way to assist the Royal Australian Air Force Lincolns from RAF Tengah to put bombs down accurately into the jungle using an Army Mobile Radar'! (It was much like the old anti-aircraft radars used during World War Two.) The radar I was given was capable of locking itself on to an over-flying aircraft and give out a slant-range readout. I had to dredge up my long forgotten schoolboy trigonometry to grapple with the system, which entailed weeks with my head in the books.

The little radar had a scanner aerial on top of a caravan and inside was a small radar screen and dials, which read off slant-range between the scanner and the aircraft. I would be in radio contact with the Lincoln, which would approach the radar from a rendezvous point at a very exact height so that the radar could pick it up. The height had to be flown very accurately by the Lincoln pilot otherwise all the calculations were void. As soon as the radar 'locked on' to the aircraft I vectored the pilot, calculated for any drift caused by the wind and ran the aircraft up to directly overhead the radar on his anticipated outbound heading. Once overhead, the radar would unlock temporarily but the Lincoln would continue on its extended track and heading until it was picked up again. At that point the run was then continued outbound on the headings given by me until the aircraft reached the computed slant-range distance on its track, at which point I gave the instruction to release the bombs.

I had to know from my map the exact location of my radar and the terrorist hideout (from photo reconnaissance pictures transposed onto my map) then measure the distance and track between the two locations. With the known horizontal distance I could work out the slant distance from my trigonometry tables to a point vertically above the target. Deducting the distance forward the bombs would travel from the point of release from the aircraft, I could come up with a bomb release point along the slant-range. As soon as the aircraft reached that point on my readout screen I instructed the Lincoln to release its bombs. After much practice in and around Singapore, the RAAF crews and I eventually got the error down to about 20 to 30 yards, which was really an incredible achievement with such primitive equipment.

The small radar caravan derived its power from an accompanying caravan with an engine driven generator and all the necessary impedimenta involved in a small mobile radar station. The inside of the scanner vehicle was rather cramped and had an air-conditioning system of sorts but, in the heat and humidity, the air conditioning system was always fighting a losing battle.

Once I had 'worked up' to a point where it was thought the idea could be used operationally, I and my accompanying technician moved 'up country' and we had a trial go 'in anger' at the terrorist camps in the Malayan jungle. I got some good results but because the project was such a success it was not long before my 'toy' was handed over to the long-term operators. I had enjoyed the challenge and would have liked to follow it through after all the hard work I had put in, but I was ordered to return to my primary duties back in Singapore.

The Far East Communication Squadron (FECS), 'B' Flight, was established to keep staff officers on ground appointments in HQ Far East Air Force (HQFEAF) in flying practice. In 1954 the flight possessed three Harvards, an Anson and an Auster and was also responsible for looking after the C-in-C's (Commander-in Chief Far East Air Force) personal Devon aircraft. Later on three Meteors 7s and two Pembrokes arrived (that's another story told later) and the Anson and Harvards were withdrawn. 'A' Flight had VIP Valettas and a venerable old York for the C-in-C on long distance visits; I scrounged a few dual training sorties in it as a co-pilot.

The Devon aircraft.

Back once more at RAF Changi, and reunited with my family, I lost no time getting back to flying with the Far East Communications Squadron. I was soon flying the Pembroke and was asked to polish up my QFI rating to convert others to that aircraft. Next, as I was qualified and competent to fly the C-in-C's Devon, I flew both successive C-in-Cs, (Air Marshal Sir Francis Fressanges followed by Air Marshal the Earl of Bandon), even though I was only

'... a venerable old York ...'

Far East Communications Squadron at RAF Changi, 1965 - VIP Valetta, Pembroke and York.

available to fly on a part-time basis. Later on, when the Meteors arrived, I also eventually shouldered the job of the Jet Aircraft Instrument Rating Examiner to add to my list of part-time duties with the Communications Squadron - i.e. in the radar unit in the morning and flying in the afternoon and vice-versa.

Just after Christmas the Chief of the Air Staff, Sir Hugh Pugh-Lloyd, arrived at Changi, personally flying a Canberra. He was horrified to find that many of the headquarters Staff Officers were planning and directing the war in Malaya involving operational jet aircraft, when most of them had not flown a jet at all, while others were not in current practice on them. He set about changing all that and, 'bingo', three Meteor Mk7 trainers became available at the Squadron almost overnight!

However a big problem immediately arose as there was no qualified Meteor instructor in FEAF and it would have taken months to organise a posting out from the UK of a suitably qualified QFI. However, I was there, an A2 Meteor flying instructor and therefore suitable and qualified, but the problem was I was officially on a ground tour and would normally be required to work at the radar station. There were many top-level conferences to try to allow me (who eagerly agreed!) to officially fly in my off-shift periods with the senior staff officers in the mornings or afternoons.

The normal SSOC shift pattern started at 6am till noon and/or noon till 6pm. This system worked for a while but as these high-ranking officers got part way into their conversions to jet flying they found they could only fly when their main staff duties permitted. As these very AVMs and Group Captains did not like to have to keep changing planning conferences and appointments, some high-level telephone calls were constantly being made to my CO to release me from my duties at other times as well! I was, of course, delighted at this, but my boss was not and he eventually got so fed up he gave up in total disgust and said 'you might as well have him all the time'!

Thus I was then posted to full flying duties at the Far East Communication Squadron just six months from the end of my overseas tour. About this time three Vampire T11s were introduced to replace the three Meteor 7s and so the conversion flying began all over again!

The amount of work involved in the flying programme on the 'Poor Man's Advanced Flying School', as it became known, meant having my overseas tour extended by six months to enable me to complete the conversion of the staff officers to the Vampire. My family and I were delighted with this as we were thoroughly enjoying the life in Singapore. I converted over 20 pilots to Meteors who had never flown them before and gave many others a refresher course - now it was starting all over again with the Vampire. It was a considerable feat involving over 600 hours flying and yet officially for the greater part of the time I was on a Ground Tour!

The Far East Air Force senior Staff Officers had good reason to be very grateful to me as they were told in no uncertain terms by the Chief of the Air Staff, when he visited, that if any one of them from the C-in-C down failed to immediately become qualified on jets they would be posted and their promotion prospects would be affected!

There were compensations and relief from the daily grind of Meteor and Vampire conversion flying in the tropical humidity.

The trainer version of the Meteor - the Mk7.

Circuit flying in a Meteor 7, which is not air-conditioned, out in Singapore was a very hot job indeed. Pilots would sweat buckets in a temperature approaching 120°F inside the 'greenhouse' cockpit canopy.

Every so often I had a welcome break when I was able to take the C-in-C and other VIPs around the Far East in the Devon. I flew to some exotic non-RAF airfields including Saigon, before the Vietnam troubles flared up. In those halcyon days one could take

Vampire T11.

one's wife on certain flights. So on one occasion I took my wife, Dorothy, to the tropical island of Car Nicobar, (mentioned in Chapter 9), way out in the Indian Ocean, and then on to Negombo, Ceylon (now Sri Lanka), for a few days' stay in the Officers' Mess there. At other times I managed to fly my wife to Hong Kong; while we were away the Amah looked after the children. Life could be quite exciting and rewarding in the Royal Air Force in those days.

My final flight in the Devon remains with me as a very pleasant memory in which I took the Earl of Perth, the Minister of State for the Colonies, and Lady Perth on a ten-day tour of Borneo.

It was just as well I did a proving flight as the wrong kind of oil was put in the engines. Fortunately the civilian engineer discovered what had been done soon after I took off from Labuan. When mineral oil and detergent oil are mixed it congeals and the engines would have seized up if I had gone much further! This kind of flying into and out of small unsophisticated jungle strips required very careful supervision on the part of the crew.

Two days later on the proving flight I then burst a tyre landing on the rough stony strip at Tawau in East Borneo. I had to find and hire a taxi and went into the local native village and borrowed

Self and navigator with the Earl and Lady Perth.

a car jack. The navigator and I got the wheel off and rushed it back to the village in the taxi to have the puncture repaired, and then finally, with great relief, got it back onto the undercarriage leg.

Only then could we move the Devon off the tiny strip to let the local Borneo Airways Rapide land. What should have been a three-day proving flight took eight days but the lessons were learnt and we were prepared for actual VIP flight.

My navigator and I set off with the Earl and his wife and, of course, everywhere we went we were feted and given VIP treatment as the Minister's crew. We enjoyed the best hotels, food and conducted tours. We received magnificent hospitality including invitations to all the cocktail parties and functions the Minister attended. The Governors of Sarawak, Sir Anthony Able, and North Borneo, Sir Roland Turnbull, joined us also as the flight progressed. We stopped over in Kuching, Sibu, Bintulu, Lutong, Brunei, Jesselton, Tawau, Sandakan and Labuan (each in itself straight out of a Somerset Maughan novel).

At Sibu we followed the VIP party up the river into the jungle to visit a 'Longhouse' and we sampled the local hospitality. This started with topless maidens swimming out to our canoe! We were given a meal of rice and meat, which tasted foul and had, by custom, to be eaten with the left hand. There were no knives, forks or spoons and it turned out the reason for using the left hand was that the right was used for toilet purposes (no toilet paper was available in the remote jungle Longhouses!)

During the meal the topless maidens selected the man they fancied and sat with him; if she shared his plate the lucky man was expected to go to bed with her! (What wonderful customs!). Dreadful tasting but diabolically strong rice wine was liberally dispensed to the guests in half coconut shells during the meal. Just as it was beginning to have a very pleasant effect and the maidens were beginning to appear even more attractive, we were bustled back into the canoe and taken back to Sibu! Borneo in those days was a delightful, tranquil and balmy part of the world with very friendly people. The beautiful tropical foliage and colourful villages, like the houses on stilts in the water at Brunei, were all unspoilt then by the Confrontation

A young Flying Officer with Dorothy and Linda at Buckingham Palace, March 1958.

War with Indonesia, which was to flare up later.

    I ended my overseas tour in the Far East on 29th September 1957 and returned to the UK accompanied by my family on a civil Hermes aircraft. The award of an Air Force Cross was promulgated on the 1st January 1958 and I am, so far as is known, the only pilot to be awarded an AFC for flying carried out on a ground tour!

Chapter 11
TEST PILOT 1957 - 1960

My next posting back in the UK after a long leave was to become a Production Test Pilot in Maintenance Command. At that time the Royal Air Force had a lot of aircraft in storage to supplement its first line strength. The aircraft were stored and repaired in Maintenance Units dotted around the country and each unit had its own Test Pilot whose job it was to test each aircraft thoroughly before it was issued to an operational unit. There was a north and south test pilots pool, the north pool at RAF Hawarden (Chester) and the south at RAF Aston Down, (near Stroud in Gloucestershire). Pilots were posted to one of the two pools for initiation and schooling in the job of a Production Test Pilot, after which they were sent out to the individual Maintenance Units for instruction on each type of aircraft held there. Once qualified to test all the types of aircraft, normally within his geographical area, a test pilot in the pool could be called upon at short notice to take over the test flying whenever the resident test pilot became sick, went on leave or on courses. I was posted to the northern pool at RAF Hawarden and my wife and children took up residence in an Officers' Married Quarter there. It goes without saying that once again this sort of job meant I was separated from my family a great deal.

Initially I was utilised as the 'taxi' pilot in the Varsity, did a jet refresher and instrument-rating course and was slowly worked up

Valetta of Ferry Training Unit and Varsity from the Test Pilots' Pool at Hawarden.

on various aircraft type conversions as mentioned above.

Once qualified, my first full relief assignment was to 23 Maintenance Unit at RAF Aldergrove in Northern Ireland, where I flew the Swift, Javelin, Canberra and Shackleton Mk3. On my third test flight in a Swift I had a most frightening experience, all because of something, which should have been explained to me during my conversion. I had just reached the top of the climb at 45,000 feet and was about to dive the Swift for a supersonic test when I noted the 'fuel dolls-eyes' were blinking and the fuel gauge reading was almost zero. I thought I had a massive fuel leak so I hurtled back to Aldergrove putting out a 'Mayday' call. By the time I was 'downwind' of the runway the fuel gauges read zero, and in my haste to keep close to the runway to get the aircraft down in case the engine stopped, I got too close. The trouble was that when the undercarriage of the Swift was selected down the nosewheel door caused the aircraft to yaw as it locked down. I left my wheels up until the last

Javelin model.

Swift Mk5.

moment and as I turned to line up with the runway in a fairly steep turn I selected them down but as the nosewheel came down it yawed the aircraft away from the runway centreline.

It was a heart-stopping decision but there was no alternative - I had missed the runway and I had to go round again! With the fuel gauges reading zero I wheeled round and tried again but was ready to eject the moment the engine showed any sign of stopping. With great relief, I landed the Swift safely next time around. What I should have been told was that the automatic fuel balancing system which kept the fuel evenly placed in the sweptback wings (to prevent the aircraft becoming tail heavy) sometimes became unserviceable, and, when it did, for some reason (which I cannot now remember) it affected the total fuel readings on the gauges; hence the reading of zero fuel when in fact the aircraft was still half full! This was a typical sort of reason why aircraft were very thoroughly tested when they come out of storage before being issued to squadrons in the

Shackleton Mk2 model.

front line.

The Maintenance Units in my northern 'parish' were RAF Stations Aldergrove, Silloth, Kirkbride, Shawbury and Hawarden, so by the middle of the year I was qualified to relieve each of the resident test pilots as and when required. Occasionally when the southern area experienced shortages I could also be called upon to help out down there too, so sometimes I could also find myself at RAF Stations Wroughton, St. Athan, Kemble, Colerne or Lyneham. At times I could be testing as many as 12 different types of aeroplanes in any one month!

One of the types I enjoyed flying was the Beverley at Shawbury. Someone once said it was like flying an airborne threshing machine - how apt - but it was

The airborne threshing machine!

strange to go from a tiny little Venom so close to the ground to being up so high in the Beverley!

One of the jobs I found myself doing at St Athan was the flight testing of the modifications to the Canberra tail trim problem that killed my friend on No.1(O) FU. It consisted of running the electric tail trim fully nose down and measuring the amount of 'pull' needed on the control column to counteract the trimmer while holding the aircraft in the straight and level mode. There had been a modification to limit and slow down the severity and amount of a runaway trimmer.

Eventually the great day came when I was given my own Maintenance Unit and I became the resident Unit Test Pilot at No. 49 MU at RAF Colerne. Colerne was shared between 49 Maintenance Unit, two Hastings squadrons of Transport Command and the Special Installations Squadron, which was concerned with the modification of any RAF aircraft by fitting special equipment of any kind. These aircraft and their new equipment had to be tested in the air, although hopefully nothing had been done that would materially affect the flying characteristics of the aeroplane. There was also a Repair and Salvage Unit belonging to the Maintenance Unit, which retrieved crashed aircraft and if possible made them airworthy again. This would entail very thorough air testing. Finally, there was the Avro Maker's Working Party carrying out inspections and repairs on Shackletons; all of which needed to be flown and tested before being re-issued to the squadrons. I realised I was in for an interesting time. I settled into my big office in the hangar and for the first time in my career had my name on the door which proudly announced to all and sundry 'Unit Test Pilot - FLT LT N E Rose AFC'. Big deal!

By now, though, I was becoming fed up with the number of times my family had been uprooted to new locations, and in particular my children's fractured education, so I decided to put down an anchor and, for the first time in my life, I bought a house - in Bath. I paid £3000 for a brand new one in 1957, although I could hardly raise the deposit of £300 at the time! Today that house is worth £300,000 or more!

My first incident in my new post was in a Shackleton. I took off from Colerne to deliver it to Langar (at that time a Royal Canadian Air Force Base) with just a flight engineer. Coming in to land, I closed the throttles but found that the No.1 engine (left outer) throttle lever would not close fully when I throttled back during 'hold-

Hastings model.

off' just before touch-down. This caused the big aeroplane to swing off the runway. I quickly retrieved what could have become a nasty situation by slamming open all four throttles and going round again. I found there was no way I could get No.1 throttle to close fully so I stopped No.1 engine, feathered the propeller and carried out an uneventful three engine landing. When the engine cowlings were opened up a spanner was found jammed in the throttle linkage stopping the throttle from

Army Prospector flown on Decca Navigator trials.

closing. It is doubtful if the culprit was ever found, but sheer negligence like that can cost aircrew lives and this particular incident might have ended up much less happily.

In June 1959, the Special Installation Squadron was tasked with fitting two Army EP 9 Prospectors with Decca Navigator equipment. These two aircraft were very highly favoured by the Army hierarchy, because they were comfortable and easy to enter and leave, and made ideal taxis for senior Generals! They were the only two aircraft of that particular type the Army Air Corps possessed and they guarded them jealously. A Major of the Army Air Corps delivered the first one to Colerne and stated his intention of returning to carry out the airborne trials. He was very promptly told that the RAF Unit Test Pilot was in charge of the trials and he would carry them out! After an inter-service stand up argument it was settled that the Unit Test Pilot would indeed do the trials so the Major gave me a short conversion flight in the aircraft (much against his injured pride!).

Three months later my navigator and I commenced the actual Decca trials and we collected the other Prospector from Middle Wallop. My claim to fame is that I am the only RAF pilot to have flown both the Army's Prospectors.

Unit Test Pilots get used to 'frighteners'. I had one while testing a Meteor T7. The aircraft developed elevator flutter and this symptom can soon cause an aircraft to break up. I put out a 'MAYDAY' call, kept the speed as low as possible and prepared to bale out. However, at the last minute, I spotted the long runway at RAF Lyneham and so, keeping the speed as low as I could, I managed to put the Meteor down on the runway. I have to say I have never baled out of an aircraft and frankly was scared of doing so, especially so as in this case it was a Meteor Mk 7, which did not have an ejector seat!

There followed an uneventful conversion to the Handley Page Hastings that would have made the venerable instructors at the Hastings OCU go grey! I was given three hours twenty minutes dual and then sent solo with just a flight engineer. I was then carrying out Hastings test flights and trials with my own maintenance unit navigator and engineer, (who, incidentally, was a ground engineer from my MU staff and not a qualified flight engineer!)

At the end of 1959 after three years in the job, I realised that all good things must come to an end and that a posting would inevitably come my way. The brand new Bristol Britannia, the most modern airliner of its time, had been purchased for Transport

Prototype Britannia G-ANCA returning from a test flight. Sadly this aircraft crashed later killing all on board. The cause was believed to have been an autopilot malfunction.

Command. Twenty three Britannias were due to enter RAF service and it had long been my ambition to fly all over the world in big four-engined aircraft as a RAF Transport Command pilot. With this in mind I applied through the normal RAF channels, without much hope of success, to achieve such a posting, but little did I realise what was about to happen!

When I was in the Far East converting pilots to jet aircraft (in Chapter 10) at RAF Changi, one of the pilots I converted to the Meteor was the Senior Personnel Staff Officer, at the time a Group Captain. The Group Captain was later promoted and became an Air Commodore holding the post of Senior Air Staff Officer at HQ Transport Command. At RAF Changi he had befriended me and we had remained in contact over the years. Obviously he must have thought something of me, because some time after applying to fly Britannias I received a letter from him informing me I had been selected for training as a Britannia captain solely at his personal recommendation. Someone 'up there' must have been watching over me!

At that period in my career it was far beyond my wildest dreams to actually be selected as a captain on Britannias straight away. It was absolutely unknown for an outsider without four-engine experience to enter Transport Command direct to the left hand seat and become a captain without having been through the 'transport' mill as a co-pilot. However, what I did not know was that I was the subject of an experiment to find out if older experienced pilots could successfully be selected from other Commands for direct captaincy on large transport aircraft!

Not long after I received the letter from the Air Commodore, a posting notice arrived instructing me to report to No.242 OCU at Dishforth, Yorkshire where I was, initially, to do the six-week Transport Command Ground School Course before commencing the very long and arduous conversion course to the Britannia.

Chapter 12
THE WHISPERING GIANT
1960 - 1963

The Transport Command Operational Conversion Unit at Dishforth was perhaps the best of its kind in the world. Before any transport crew members stepped into an aeroplane they were subjected to eight weeks solid grind in the ground school. One subject, which was superbly dealt with was global climatology that really gave the pilot an excellent knowledge of world weather. It enabled him to understand and cope with vastly different climates that he would encounter round the world. The long range transport crews would have to fly in conditions varying from ice and snow to scorching desert winds, from freezing rain and hail to tropical hurricanes, from fog to mirages, from violent thunderstorms to clear air turbulence, from arctic fog to the intertropical convergence zones, from St Elmo's fire to airframe icing - and the many other hazards which Nature's weather can fling at the aviator from time to time.

After the final examinations at RAF Dishforth, I reported back to RAF Lyneham to attend the Britannia ground school. During the next 12 weeks I learned just about everything there was to know about the Britannia on one of the most comprehensive courses I have ever attended. The Britannia was one of the first 'electronic' aeroplanes of its kind and was an electrical nightmare to the uninitiated aircrews. It was, however, a pleasant course at the Bristol Aeroplane factory at Filton and the tuition was first class. The crews all seemed to possess a great sense of humour and this helped to overcome the boredom which crept in during the more stuffy technical lectures! Lunchtimes were looked forward to especially as the Company gave us two bottles of beer each and a superb meal every day. Presumably it was all covered in the price of each aircraft sold to the RAF! By the end of 12 weeks, we all knew every nut, bolt, and every amp and volt around what, at the time was a very big and sophisticated aeroplane.

On my return to Lyneham once more, I settled into yet another lot of ground school lectures for three weeks. Now we concentrated more on RAF operating techniques and etched forever in my memory were the immortal words of the instructor regarding an engine fire on take-off in a Britannia - 'Don't rush things - sit and have a fag and a Kit-Kat before taking any action!' How right he was! It was much more probable that a stupid and possibly fatal error could be made by panicing into the fire drill on take-off, whereas the situation would not deteriorate dramatically by tackling it thoughtfully and carefully.

There now followed 30 hours instruction in the Britannia simulator until eventually the crews started flying together. Until this time only the two pilots and the flight engineer had trained together. Now our navigators, air quartermasters and signallers joined us for in-flight training. After 14 hours 20 minutes dual I was sent off on my own with my crew. It was an exhilarating feeling to be in sole charge of such a big and beautiful aeroplane.

I then spent endless hours learning 'every which way' of the

Model making continues - and they don't get much bigger than the Britannia!

Britannia in the air including instrument letdowns, three and two-engined landings, three-engined take-offs, followed by a route trainer to Singapore with an instructor. Finally, I had protracted ground examinations and comprehensive air examinations (called 'Categorisation') involving day and night checks and instrument flying.

My final 'solo' trainer was to Nicosia in Cyprus and was my indoctrination to some of the dangers which weather could bring. On my approach to Nicosia at night a very large thunderstorm was flashing away over the nearby mountains. We were in cloud using the only navigational aid available on the ground, i.e. the Non-Directional Beacon, to approach the airfield, but unknown to us the needle of the Automatic Direction Finder in the aircraft pointed to the centre of the storm over the mountain instead of at the airfield beacon (a common problem with the automatic direction finder). The navigator only discovered the problem at the last minute but it taught me a lesson, never trust aircraft instruments implicitly when thunderstorms are around! On that occasion it could have led us to crash into the mountain and no one would probably have known why. I have always remembered this incident, how dangerous weather conditions can be, throughout my flying career.

In those early days of accustoming myself to the rigours of route flying, particularly the problem of sleeping by day to get up and fly by night, many of the more experienced 'old soldiers' tried to pass on to me their ideas of how to cope with it. On one of my early flights I was sharing a room with my navigator (not my usual one) and we were scheduled to take-off at around 2200 hrs (Aden time), which meant trying to sleep in the afternoon. The navigator said he always had a lunchtime beer drinking session, which put him to sleep in the afternoon so he departed leaving me trying desperately to get to sleep in our room after lunch. At around three o'clock the navigator came staggering into the room flung himself on his bed fully clothed and after a short while complained that the room was 'going round and round' then rushed over to the sink and was sick! He spent the rest of the afternoon alternating between the sink and his bed complaining loudly how ill he felt! As a result I was unable to get a wink of sleep that afternoon. The navigator went to pre-flight briefing as white as a sheet and felt ill all the way home and I fell asleep at the controls at one point during the double leg to the UK via El Adem, arriving at dawn in the UK! This was a piece of route flying 'advice' I decided was not on!

Although crew members were not regularly assigned to a particular captain, they were able to assess individual captain's skills and his 'Captaincy' both on the ground and in the air. So when the monthly tasking went up in the various offices, with a captain's name allotted, they were able to request to fly with the captain of their choice. I was quite proud of the fact that my regular co-pilot, navigator, flight engineer and signaller always loyally asked to stay with me. What eventually resulted from this was our nickname. We were all of small stature, somewhat rotund, and certainly no oil paintings, so we became affectionately known throughout the Britannia world as the 'smallest and ugliest crew in the fleet'!

Many months later I was allotted an aero-medical flight from Singapore. As soon as I positioned there with my crew, I was sent for by the RAF Hospital at Changi to be briefed on the medical requirements for the flight we were to operate back to the UK. I was introduced to the doctors and the sisters who made up the medical team on board the aircraft and was given details of the in-flight requirements. For aero-medical flights most of the Britannia's seats were removed to allow stretchers to be installed and no effort was spared to ensure that the patients received superb care throughout their flight back to UK. My crew and I geared ourselves to operate the aircraft in a manner least likely to upset the patients. This meant avoiding bad weather and ensuring that general handling and especially landings were really smooth. Take-offs were not started unless the destination with hospital facilities could be safely reached. Any special requirements such as pressurisation and ventilation had to be observed. It was vitally important in this particular case to avoid any form of turbulence, as one patient was a lady with a broken back who was also eight months pregnant!

Whilst it was still relatively cool in the early morning, the patients were loaded on to a specially cooled aircraft. In the tropics the Britannia became very hot inside the fuselage while it was on the ground, (the aircraft's ventilation and cooling system did not operate until the engines were running). So it was necessary to get a priority clearance from Air Traffic Control to get started and airborne as quickly as possible. This was done before the ground coolers were removed.

On landing at Gan we heard strange rumours that Iraq was threatening to invade Kuwait. When there was a flare-up in the world involving RAF Transport Command, the first thing to happen was that the Britannias were withdrawn from the 'bread and butter' scheduled services to operate transporting men and materials to the trouble spots. This, in fact, was what was happening. But to an aero-medical flight - we were intrigued!

On the 19th June 1961, oil-rich Kuwait ceased to be a British Protectorate and was recognised by Britain as a fully independent state. Iraq, however, was pressing claims to the territory of Kuwait

Britannia troop loading on another occasion.

and an armed conflict was looming. The Ruler, or Emir, of Kuwait asked for help from the British but at the time the Britannia crews overseas were blissfully unaware of the political situation.

During the approach into RAF Khormaksar, just as my crew and I were looking forward to a few ice-cold beers in 'Neddies" bar (the nickname of the airfield terminal bar so called after the Wing Commander Ops - more of that later), we were told that our aero-medical flight was terminating at Aden. We were also informed we were on immediate standby, which of course meant no ice-cold beers! We were perplexed to know what it could all be about. All became clear after a briefing by the Operations Officer and we were sent straight to bed - but we were due for a rude awakening! It was incredible that an aero-medical flight had been stopped at Khormaksar and all the patients off-loaded to the RAF Hospital in Aden especially in view of the very sick lady. It was obvious, therefore, that this was a most serious international emergency to interrupt a medical emergency such as ours.

On 1st July 1961 the first British troops were rushed to Kuwait from Aden in my aircraft with thousands more to follow from the UK. Those troops stayed until relieved by Arab League troops. Operation Vantage had begun!

Chapter 13
OPERATION VANTAGE - 1961

Four hours after going to bed, at about 1.00 am Aden time, that rude awakening arrived! I was told that my crew was to take troops to Kuwait at once. I immediately went to wake my co-pilot who refused to believe that he had to rise after only four hours in bed. Bear in mind that we had just completed a 19-hour crew duty day. In the end I had to issue an order to him to get up and remonstrated with him that this was an emergency and that legal crew rest time just went 'out of the window'.

Bleary eyed, we went to an operational briefing at 2 o'clock in the morning to be told the political situation with Kuwait and what our task was to be. We were to take 115 fully armed paratroops into a new and unknown airfield somewhere near Kuwait City. There were no maps of this new airfield, no navigational aids, no met forecast, in fact nothing! It was just 'go'! No diplomatic clearances were available either which meant we had to fly *incognito*, maintaining radio silence and with no lights showing. In fact, if the worst came to the worst we could be shot at over Saudi Arabia!

We rumbled off from Khormaksar in total darkness and five and a half hours later were talking to the civilian controllers at Kuwait International Airport.

In the early morning a strong wind was blowing across the desert and the temperature was 44°C (111°F), just one degree under the maximum temperature at which the Britannia was cleared to operate by its Certificate of Airworthiness. The visibility in the blowing sand was down to about one mile and we had absolutely no idea where the new airfield was. Kuwait International told us over the radio to fly overhead and then steer the heading given for 18 nautical miles, but with visibility so limited by the blowing sand and no maps I dared not risk flying too low. We eventually found the strip of concrete set in the sand and landed after a 'fighter style' circuit to keep the runway in sight.

On the flight to Kuwait the paratroops' Commanding Officer, a Lieutenant Colonel, his face blackened and raring to go, had been telling us that he did not know what to expect when we arrived. It was possible that the airfield would be in enemy hands, so his troops might have to fight their way off the aircraft! I began to think hard about whether I ought to risk one of her Majesty's very expensive aeroplanes in view of this charming bit of information! In the event it turned out to be a lack of communications at Aden because there was a squadron of Hunter aircraft already on the airfield. I suspected the Lieutenant Colonel was very disappointed there was no need for his men to storm their way off the aeroplane but it was a very great relief to us!. As soon as the engines stopped, my very feminine little Women's Royal Air Force air quartermaster took charge and threw out all the emergency evacuation chutes, as there were no steps available. She shouted and cajoled the tough warlike Paras down the chutes in all their battle gear and loaded rifles!

I left my crew busy retrieving the escape chutes and preparing for a quick departure. On top of the heat problem and the sand blowing everywhere, there was no fuel available and suddenly there was another extremely desperate problem - the aircraft was sinking! The flight engineer was horrified and could not believe his eyes when he saw a neat square crack appearing round the whole of the main wheel bogies and the nose wheels. The squares of concrete under the wheels were slowly descending somewhat like a lift! He yelled in desperation over to me at the Hunter dispersal, 'Captain, take a look at this, she's sinking! Let's get out of here quick!' We had to climb back into the aircraft through the front freight hatch (no mean task!) and carried out the quickest internal start of all time! The RAF Britannia was basically a civilian aircraft, which required external ground starting equipment and as we did not have an auxiliary power unit on board for internal starting, our start depended entirely on well-charged aircraft batteries. If they were not charged enough the No.3 engine (which housed the alternator to start the rest of the engines) would not turn over and ignite. Fortunately it did start and we uncrossed our fingers! Had it not started it is possible the Britannia might have sunk so far into the tarmac that it might have to be lifted out by crane. The problem was that the dispersal concrete had not been constructed deep or thick enough to support the weight of a big aeroplane like the Britannia, even when it was empty!

With just the inboard No.2 and 3 engines running, I opened up to full power and luck was with me, I managed to drag the Britannia wheels out of the holes. It was like jumping the chocks! Had I left it any longer the holes would have been too deep to get out. The outboard engines were started by my flight engineer as we taxyed. The navigator was worried sick as he did not know the length of the runway and the temperature had reached 48°C, which was well outside the maximum operating limits of the aircraft. However, I told him I was going to take-off come what may. I calculated that as the aircraft no longer had its load of passengers and barely had enough fuel to reach Bahrain, it was comparatively light and the runway had looked long enough when we landed. I also felt I must get away to warn the other incoming Britannia crews of the dangers of sinking through the concrete dispersal area.

I instructed my signaller to get on his long-range radio and report the problem to Aden and HQ Transport Command in UK. I told him to recommend that all the rest of the incoming Britannias unloaded their troops on the loops at the ends of the runway, which seemed strong enough to support the weight of the Britannia. In fact, for the rest of the period of 'Operation Vantage' the Britannia's did unload on the loops.

We had a moment of anxiety on the take-off run because the Britannia's rate of acceleration was very slow, and it wouldn't easily lift off the runway due to the extremely high temperature, but in the end we had plenty of runway left to get airborne.

About four hours later, in the circuit at Bahrain, we looked down at an airport beginning to fill up with Beverleys and Hastings of the Middle East Air Force, all being loaded up as quickly as possible for the run into Kuwait. Fortunately we were refuelled at once because we used kerosene instead of petrol so we were soon on our way back to Aden. We had been on duty for almost 30 hours since leaving Singapore with just three and a half hours in bed. We debriefed our story at Aden and by midnight (Aden time) we were all out for the count. By 9am that same morning we were off to Kuwait again.

By now a massive airlift was under way. Britannias and Hastings were pouring in from the UK. Crews were sleeping anywhere they could lay their heads. In Aden and Bahrain some were on billiard tables, some were on the floor or in hard chairs, only the lucky ones got beds. As soon as a crew arrived they woke their relief crew and got straight into the still warm spot!

My crew and I thundered, fully ladened, down the Khormaksar runway once more and set off for Kuwait. This time we knew what to expect. Transport Command HQ at Upavon had despatched an Operational Cell to organise and run things at Kuwait. They were passengers in my aircraft so I was able to give them a fairly thorough brief on the conditions they could expect.

On Day 2 of Operation Vantage, in a temperature around 45°C and in blowing sand, we arrived at the Kuwait Airfield again and disgorged our passengers and freight on the pan at the end of the runway. This time they had some makeshift steps that had just been brought in by a Beverley from Bahrain.

By now refuelling at Bahrain was a real headache with so many aircraft involved in the Operation but this is what Transport Command was (and still is) all about - to be there, ready, able, willing, eager and fully trained for anything that might arise anywhere in the world. A good example of the determination and morale of the crews was shown that evening where literally scores of aircraft were landing to refuel after going into Kuwait. Flight engineers were resorting to sheer cunning to get away again as soon as possible. If a tanker was not obtained quickly it meant a long wait in the heat and also the possibility of running out of crew duty time (supposed to be 19 hours in one day). By Day 2, Transport Command HQ had firmly clamped the rules back on so none of the crews wanted to run out of crew duty time at Bahrain and sleep on the sand or in the aircraft. So some rather devious and foul deeds, in some cases even fisticuffs, were indulged by flight engineers to divert the refuellers to their own aircraft. *Esprit de corps* went out of the window on the Bahrain dispersal and it was every crew for itself!

At the end of Day 3 we landed wearily back at Khormaksar. We had been 26 hours in the air with only ten hours sleep. We were relieved to learn we had been withdrawn from Operation Vantage. It was nearly over anyway as Iraq had come to realise that Britain was as good as its word and would back it with force, so they consequently decided that discretion was the better part of valour and backed down.

Throughout those previous three days, little WRAF Sgt Sylvia Wapen, my air quartermaster, had done a marvellous job. She had kept her 'small and ugly' flight deck crew fed and 'watered' in the air, meticulously attended to her soldier passengers, and worked very hard unloading the aircraft under the most trying conditions of searing heat and blowing sand. I cannot praise her enough for her loyal efforts during the flare-up.

A day later we left Aden for a night flight to Nairobi. During this flight we witnessed a sight none of us had seen before. Flying in medium cloud at 20,000 feet we ran into turbulence and the cloud thickened. Suddenly enormous tongues of what looked like fire licked forward some ten to fifteen feet in front of the aircraft accompanied by myriads of tiny electrical sparks playing over the windscreen. It lit up the inside of the flight deck as if it was daylight. It was a fantastic sight and yet a little frightening - St Elmo's Fire.

After landing at Nairobi, we were able to relax in comfort at the Spread Eagle Hotel and we indulged in a little party that night and swapped our individual experiences. The next evening we departed for a night flight back to the UK.

The following story came to light a fortnight after we got home. Sylvia had bought a Mynah bird in Singapore. It had sat happily in flight squawking in its rattan cage hung from the aircraft roof and was gradually learning to talk. The Mynah bird is much like a parrot in that it soon learns to imitate and 'speak', especially if encouraged with tit-bits! During Operation Vantage it had obviously picked up a lot of bad language as the bored soldiers spent their time giving the little bird tit-bits and teaching it swear words!

Sylvia had planned to be married soon after her arrival back in UK, and the local vicar came to visit her at her home to talk over her wedding arrangements. During his visit Sylvia became most embarrassed when her bird issued a few choice swear words at the vicar! She blamed it on those bawdy soldiers during the long flights to Kuwait on Operation Vantage!

There was a horrific incident during Operation Vantage, which marred an otherwise brilliant chapter of events for the 'Whispering Giant'. One night, in the confusion at Kuwait, an airman was waving his illuminated taxying wands marshalling a Britannia backwards into a space and signalling the Captain to reverse. By reversing the propeller pitch and applying a little power the Britannia could taxi backwards; however, if the pilot applied the brakes to stop the backward movement it could make the tail fall down on to the ground and could cause considerable damage, therefore, to stop rearward movement, the pilot had to cancel the reverse propeller and power and not use brake. The propeller blades then turned to give forward thrust. As a result the aircraft then started to roll forward and as soon as the pilot felt this he applied the brakes and halted the aircraft in the normal manner. It seemed possible that the poor airman was not aware of this procedure or that this could happen. So as he walked forward closely following the reversing aircraft he gave the pilot the signal to stop, but as soon as he did so the aircraft stopped reversing but immediately moved forward and the marshaller was hit and killed instantly by a propeller before the pilot could stop. It was a sad incident that served to remind ground and aircrews how careful they had to be when manoeuvring with ground crews who may not be familiar with marshalling a Britannia, as this poor airman wasn't. Even though the pilot was not to blame it left a cloud of sorrow over an otherwise excellent operation.

Chapter 14

'NEDDIES BAR' AND LIFE IN BERLIN - 1962

After Operation Vantage, my crew and I had two weeks rest and some routine training. I then did a couple of ten-day detachments in Aden as part of the 'East of Aden Policy'. Two Britannias were always on standby there and it was considered to be a sort of an enforced but much appreciated holiday, living in the civilian Rock Hotel, swimming on the beach at the Tarshyne Officers' Club and doing very little flying.

At the RAF base there was an infamous NAAFI bar, which never shut, located in the Air Movements building. It was solely there to cater for incoming aircraft crews who were operating round the clock. It was nicknamed 'Neddies Bar' after an equally infamous and volatile Wing Commander Ops (mentioned below) who presided at that time. The crews were able to walk in from their aircraft and sit down to have a 'wind-down' beer (or two!) at any hour of the day or night. It helped them to sleep after a 19-hour duty day.

One night after a long haul, double-leg flog from the UK and a couple of hours in 'Neddies Bar', my crew and I departed, at around 4 o'clock in the morning, in the crew bus to a hotel in downtown Aden. Dog-tired and ready for sleep we found the hotel had no rooms for us so we were forced to 'phone for the crew bus to return (a half hour run each way). Upon arrival back at 'Neddies Bar' we were now informed that there was nowhere else for us to sleep so we

'The smallest and ugliest Britannia crew'

sat and consumed a few more beers as dawn came up and waited for Operations to sort things out!

By this time I had had enough and told the Operations Officer on duty that I was going to complain to HQ Transport Command about this extremely tardy and shambolic organisation. Shortly after a very irate Wing Commander Ops appeared, obviously informed of the situation. He must have taken leave of his senses as he blasphemed and shouted, saying that, 'Britannia crews are a b****y nuisance,' and ordered (and I mean 'ordered'!) me and my crew to, 'get back in your aeroplane and 'b****r off back to the UK.' After a 19-hour day and drinking alcohol this was a totally illegal order. (We were not 'slipping' at Aden but were returning to UK with the same aircraft after a 15 hours rest period - or so it should have been!)

This was an order that, legally, could very obviously not be obeyed but at the same time it was a Court Martial offence to disobey an order from a senior officer. I was 'gob smacked' by his attitude and thought about it for a few minutes while the seething Wing Commander continued to rant and rave; he seemed almost demented. There was no alternative so I refused the order point blank at which the Wing Commander became absolutely incandescent. I also told the Wing Co that our 15-hour rest would only commence when beds had been found for us to sleep on and further I was going to make a formal complaint in writing to his UK HQ. Meanwhile, accommodation was very rapidly found by the Operations staff in another hotel for us, but it was nearly midday before we got to bed! The raging Wing Commander disappeared and was not seen again. The situation was made worse for him as a VIP passenger on my return flight was none other than the wife of the Commander-in-Chief of Transport Command. She enquired after take-off why the flight had been delayed so long from its scheduled take-off time and

Busy RAF Lyneham - a Britannia is being prepared for the flight to Singapore.

was told the truth! You can be sure she bent hubby's ear when she got home! I do not know what happened to the Wing Commander but he was not there the next time I went through Aden!

On another occasion, at RAF Khormaksar, an incoming 'slip' captain told me he had found his Britannia hard to get off the ground at Changi and Gan and he thought it was not performing to the ODMs (Operating Data Manuals). He had a few theories, one of which was that it had been raining heavily at Singapore and the kit of the 100 soldiers aboard had got soaked during loading and was therefore heavier than when it was originally weighed or else the freight had not been weighed correctly at Changi.

Since the runway at Khormaksar was quite short and the temperature was very hot, (which affected the engine performance), I decided to have the load re-weighed. It was just as well because the aircraft was found to be several thousand pounds over the maximum take-off weight permitted for the runway length and conditions prevailing at Khormaksar. Less fuel could not be carried so a lot of the freight including some of the soldiers' kit had to be left behind to reduce to the maximum all-up weight allowed for the aircraft. If this had not been done it is possible there would have been a terrible accident through the aircraft not getting airborne by the end of the runway.

On the same flight, at the next stop at RAF El Adem, after take-off an engine failed and the propeller had to be feathered. I turned back to El Adem and I prepared the aircraft and passengers for the jettisoning of fuel from the wing tanks to get the aircraft down to landing weight. The two jettison pipes were lowered together electrically behind each wing and valves are opened to allow the fuel to stream out safely away from the engines. It was a drill my crew knew backwards and had practised many times in the simulator. But alas, one of our jettison pipes refused to lower. The problem now was that once lowered a jettison pipe could not be retracted! If we jettisoned from one side only the aircraft would become out of balance laterally and thus dangerous to land. If we did not jettison, it would take about four hours to burn off enough fuel to get down to the permitted landing weight. After due consideration, and with my flight engineers agreement, I decided to jettison fuel from the good wing to a

BEA Viscount model.

point where it would not upset the balance too much and then transfer the fuel across from the other wing - a long winded process. It took nearly two hours before the Britannia was down to landing weight, and also within lateral control limits, before I could land back at El Adem for an engine change.

During 1962 a disagreement between the USSR and the Western Powers over Berlin resulted in a threat to shoot down civil aircraft using the air corridors into and out of Berlin. In turn this meant that BEA (British European Airways) crews were not covered for insurance, so the RAF was called in to operate the Viscounts in the corridors. As a result several Britannia crews were selected to be trained on the Viscount. In the event of trouble flaring up those crews would take over and keep them flying to maintain air access into and out of Berlin, possibly with a fighter escort!

With a co-pilot I went to the BEA ground school at Cranford and did a week's instruction and simulator training. This was followed by flying instruction on the Viscount at Heathrow and Stanstead. In August I went out in civilian clothes to Templehof in Berlin for a week and operated alongside BEA crews up and down the corridors to Hanover and Hamburg and were looked after and fed every lunchtime by the gorgeous German female cabin crews. I found this a different world altogether and the life style certainly appealed to me. I lived in luxury at the Hotel Kempinsky in the centre of Berlin, all paid for by BEA. On top of that I was given advance allowances of £3.50 a day in German currency. At that time, to the RAF, this was an astronomical sum of money to feed ourselves. It meant I could live well, eat well, see Berlin by day while I was not flying, and even paid for my drinks all night! Hardships! Typically though, afterwards the RAF accountants got hot under the collar about this when they got the bill from BEA and made all the RAF crews involved sign a document to say they spent all their allowances on food! And guess what - with tongue in cheek, we all did!

After seeing at first hand how the other half lived (i.e. civilian airline pilots), for the first time in my life I began to wonder whether to leave the austere and poorly paid RAF life to join the ranks of those well-paid and pampered pilots who, after all, did the same job!

Chapter 15
FLYING VIPs and TROUBLE IN BEIRUT

I gradually worked my way up the Strategic Transport Pilot Category ladder until I reached a 'B' Category and managed to get selected for a 'VIP' endorsement - quite an achievement (even if I say so myself) considering that just two years previously I was the most junior and inexperienced four-engined transport pilot in the Britannia fleet. My first VIP flight was with Lord Ian Orr-Ewing, the Civil Lord of the Admiralty, taking him, his wife and private secretary to Aden and Singapore.

On the first leg, flying in a cloudless blue sky over France, Lady Orr-Ewing was stood up on the flight deck admiring the scenery of the snow capped Alps when suddenly we encountered a strange phenomena - without warning the aircraft struck clear air turbulence for a few seconds. The great Britannia lurched and fell lifting Lady Orr-Ewing off her feet and she struck her head on the roof. Fortunately she was not seriously hurt but it shook her up a bit as well as everyone else on board. I had never before, and never since, experienced such a frightening, unexplained and unexpected occurrence.

Next, as captain of a flight to the United States, I was privileged to spend two days at Andrews Air Force Base, Washington DC. My crew and I were taken inside 'AIR FORCE ONE', the President's aircraft, and were treated, courtesy of the USAF, to a tour of Washington DC. We also had night stops in Chicago, Los Angeles (a day out at Disneyland), New Orleans (a visit to the French Quarter) and Las Vegas (a visit to Frank Sinatra's Caesars Palace for a little flutter!). Indescribable hardships!

In May, I was allocated a worldwide VIP flight lasting a month. The VIP was the Air Member for Supply and Organisation, Air Marshal Sir Jack Davis CB, OBE, affectionately known as 'Iron Jaw Jack'. The trip started badly because some 'kind' person in MOD gave the senior air quartermaster the wrong information on what wine the Air Marshal liked to drink with his meals. Leibfraumilch Blue Nuns was confidently given as his favourite but when it was served with his first meal the poor air quartermaster was given a flea in his ear because the Air Marshal hated the stuff! (We gallantly consumed it all on his behalf during our night stops! - thankyou Iron Jaw!)

The first leg was a non-stop flight from RAF Lyneham to

At the Britannia controls - inevitably at night!

Nairobi with a scheduled 'doors closed/doors open' time of 14 hours. This was achieved by climbing the Britannia to the top of its flight envelope of 35,000 feet to conserve fuel. It was the longest non-stop flight I have ever undertaken in my lengthy flying career. It was also probably the longest scheduled Britannia flight in RAF history and could possibly have qualified for the Guinness Book of Records. There were a total of 15 flight sectors to the assignment and I was proud of the fact that every landing was dead on time. The faithful Britannia never let me down and my navigator was almost a miracle worker in the way he steered us through nights and days and bad weather so accurately, and he wasn't a second out with his arrival times!

The only hiccup in what was otherwise a perfect VIP flight was at Hong Kong. The Air Marshal bought a beautiful camphor-wood chest and had it delivered to the Air Movements Section at RAF Kai Tak. His faithful corporal travelling with him tried to take charge of the loading of the chest with the rest of his boss's kit but the Air Movement's corporal was having none of that! The unfortunate outcome was that during the loading of the chest, it was gouged badly down one side.

After the Air Marshal came on board, his terrified corporal told the Air Marshal's Personal Staff Officer, a Squadron Leader, what had happened. The staff officer paled under his tan but delayed telling his boss until they were airborne. I was then sent for as soon as we reached 'top of the climb' and I received one of the biggest 'bollockings' of my life. 'Iron Jaw' never repeated himself once and made it ever so clear to me that I should have supervised the loading of the chest personally. There seemed little point in my reminding the Air Marshal that I, as the captain, had to go to flight planning and oversee every aspect of the forthcoming flight or that it was not my responsibility to actually load the aircraft as that there was a qualified Air Movements staff to supervise that. I wisely thought the less said the better in view of the Air Marshal's anger! The staff officer and the corporal had retreated to the rear and Lady Davis just sat there looking quietly amused at the apoplectic antics of her enraged husband! The Air Marshal then scribbled a signal to the AOC Hong

Kong telling him what he though of Kai Tak Movements staff. I still wonder if anyone was 'beheaded' at RAF Kai Tak!

After landing at Changi the ground crew witnessed an incredible and unbelievable sight never before seen of a Britannia captain and his co-pilot, dressed in their specially issued VIP dress uniforms, personally and very, very carefully shifting a camphorwood chest into the back of the aircraft front freight bay and securing it in a safe place!

Until the incident with the chest the Air Marshal had been very friendly towards us and as he was a pilot he had enjoyed a few hours each leg on the flight deck flying the aircraft himself. The flight from Hong Kong to Changi was strained to say the least and he was not seen up front. After four days in Singapore he had obviously cooled down and came to the flight deck on the way to Gan. He was quite his old self again and asked to resume flying the aircraft. From then on it was roses (excuse the pun!) all the way and the chest was never mentioned again until we reached the UK. After our final landing there the Air Marshal's language was unprintable when, to add insult to injury, he was charged duty on his damaged chest by the Customs Officer at RAF Lyneham. He was not a happy bunny! Despite his camphorwood chest I received a thankyou letter from him a few days later and there was no mention of it!

My next VIP flight was to fetch Admiral Sir Peter and Lady Hill-Norton back from Singapore at the completion of his tour of duty as Commander-in-Chief Far East. VIP flights were always a joy to fly because take-offs were at such nice respectable times in the morning, and the crew did not 'slip' but always remained with the aircraft. Whenever a Britannia went 'off-route' i.e. to airfields where normal RAF servicing was not available, a SNCO ground engineer would be carried as a crew member. These engineers (called crew chiefs) did a stalwart job and worked extremely hard as they flew all day with the aircraft but when the crew went off to have a beer and relax at the end of the day the crew chief started his work refuelling, servicing and readying the aircraft for next day. He cleaned the cabin, put the aircraft to 'bed' and if there was a 'snag' (unserviceability) or a problem with the aircraft he would often be up all night. He was then obliged to try to snatch some sleep after take-off in one of the seats on board. They were long suffering but cheerful men upon whom captains and flight engineers depended completely.

Admiral Sir Peter Hill-Norton was a very popular Commander-in-Chief in the Far East so there was a very poignant ceremonial departure for him. The sad and tearful farewell at the bottom of the steps at RAF Changi inevitably delayed the closing of the rear door of the aircraft by 15 minutes. In all good VIP flight planning a bit of 'fat' is added to the flight plan time to allow for such contingencies so we were able to arrive dead on scheduled 'doors-open' time at Gan. It is to the credit of my crew and to the crew chief that the final arrival at Gatwick was also dead on time.

An incident, which illustrates what a superb man the Admiral was to work for, happened at Masirah. He asked me and my crew to join him for drinks in the Officers' Mess and to bring his Marine Corporal driver as it was the corporal's birthday! The Admiral made a speech thanking his corporal for his many years of faithful service

With Admiral of the Fleet, Lord Hill-Norton and wife. I'm the fat one, fourth from the right!

as his driver and announced that he would continue to serve him in the same capacity when he took up his new appointment as Chief of the Defence Staff. Firstly, he publicly promoted him to Sergeant but the *pièce de résistance* followed when the Admiral presented him with a set of keys to a brand new Mini Clubman as a birthday present that would be waiting for him at Gatwick! Lady Hill-Norton presented him with a most beautiful filigree silver table lighter. Needless to say the corporal was overwhelmed and totally flabbergasted. It was an occasion, which brought a lump to my throat and has remained in my mind as the sort of thing that highlights all that is best in the Armed Forces and certainly made me feel proud to be a part.

In June, I was waiting at RAF Akrotiri (Cyprus) on the way home from the Changi Slip when a crisis in Lebanon blew up. Instead of taking the next aircraft on to UK when it arrived, it was turned around and I was diverted in it to Beirut to pick up the British Embassy staff. As I taxied into the dispersal at Beirut the aircraft suddenly sprang a hydraulic leak. The first that I realised I had a problem was when the hydraulic warning light came on and, simultaneously, I had brake failure. Since I was very close to and heading straight towards a terminal building something had to be done quickly. Instantaneously I ordered, 'Engineer, brake failure drill', just as we had been taught in the simulator back at Lyneham.

The only way to stop a Britannia with all four engines running when the brakes fail is to put two engines into full reverse with the other two idling in forward pitch and then by judicious juggling the flight engineer, who handles the throttles all the time, can halt the aircraft. Unfortunately, at that moment, only the two inboard engines were running. (It was standard drill to shut down the two outboard engines after landing to prevent constant use of brakes to stop the aircraft accelerating, especially when the aircraft is light, thus preventing excessive wear and over heating to the brakes) It is fortunate that the engineer was very experienced because he quickly put both the engines into reverse to stop the aircraft from hitting the building then backed it off a few feet and juggled the individual engines in forward and reverse to hold the aircraft still until the crew chief could scramble down through the front freight hatch, obtain some chocks and chock the wheels so that I could shut down the engines. It was a near thing but I had the highest praise for my flight engineer's outstanding quick handling of what could have become a serious accident especially in view of the political situation pertaining at the time.

The situation on the ground at Beirut was a bit chaotic and little cooperation could be obtained. In the end the flight engineer and the crew chief unscrewed the offending piece of hydraulic pipe from the aircraft and disappeared into the town in a taxi! About two hours later they reappeared clutching two pieces of pipe - the old one and the other they had made themselves! 'Best you don't ask too much about it,' they said with grins on their faces. They had gone into town and into a little Kasbah workshop, borrowed the two local Arabs tools and forged the pipe! Superb initiative!

During the wait I had contacted Akrotiri Ops on the Single Side Band High Frequency radio and explained my predicament. The British were not too popular in Beirut at that time and the situation was somewhat tense particularly for the refugees from the British Embassy I had come to rescue. I made contact with them and got them on board as soon as the two engineers reappeared with the new pipe. They explained that it would be an emergency 'get you home' measure. I was quite happy with that and decided to fly the short distance across to Cyprus with the wheels locked down to avoid using the hydraulics. Normally the hydraulic system would have to be primed and cycled before it could be declared serviceable to fly and raise and lower the undercarriage, but this was an emergency!

The two engineers installed the pipe, and replenished the hydraulic tank with fluid and ran an engine to build up the pressure. The brakes seemed OK so I decided to leave as soon as possible. I was just about to depart when Akrotiri Ops came up on the radio to say they had mobilised another Britannia and it would be on its way in three or four hours. I told Ops of my intentions to return with my passengers with the wheels locked down (with the local pipe modification installed) but after a long pause (obviously passed up the line for higher consideration) I was told I could return in that mode but not carrying passengers. It seemed a strange decision considering the current situation on the ground at Beirut. My crew and I returned to RAF Akrotiri with the empty aircraft where the ground engineers declared the pipe and its installation to be better than the original!

Perhaps my first real introduction to the age-old adage, that a 'long range transport pilot's life consists of hours and hours of boredom interspersed with moments of sheer terror', was out in the middle of the Atlantic Ocean on my way to Gander. The calm and quiet of the flight deck was suddenly broken by the strident fire alarm bell indicating a fire in No.2 engine. The bell was cancelled and the fire drill was rapidly carried out by the flight engineer but the fire warning light remained on after the pre-requisite 30 seconds, (panic stations!); so the second shot was pressed but the light still remained on after a further 30 seconds indicating that the fire had not been extinguished! (Greater panic!). By using the second shot it meant we now had no fire protection on the adjacent No.1 engine as it was used up on No.2 engine. Although the flight engineer could not see any sign of fire visually it did not necessarily mean the fire was out. We put out a 'MAYDAY' and I thought about our prospects as I did not relish a wing on fire!. I asked the Nav for the position of the nearest Ocean Station Weather Ship in case we had to ditch which, thankfully, was quite close by. However, I decided to play it cool and hoped it was a false alarm. After about ten minutes there was still no external signs of fire so we headed for the UK and cancelled the MAYDAY. To cut a long story short we got back OK and the cause was found to be a short circuit in the fire warning electrical system. I now knew what was meant by that adage! Incidentally, in all the time I spent on Britannias I never heard of another case like this one.

Chapter 16
THE FREIGHT HOLD FIRE
NOVEMBER 1962

At about two o' clock in the morning on 15th November, 1962, Britannia XL636 (the oldest in the Fleet) was cruising in the inky blackness about 100 nautical miles north of Rome heading along the airway to Elba and the UK. One hundred passengers were asleep in the cabin and all was quiet. Suddenly the strident fire alarm bell rang out on the flight deck and the red fire warning light lit up indicating fire in the front freight hold. My crew and I immediately carried out the fire drill exactly as we had done so many times in the simulator. At the same time smoke began to pour into the flight deck and I ordered my crew to put on their oxygen masks and told the flight engineer to go and investigate. The signaller was instructed to call Rome Control and warn them that we might need to descend quickly to a height at which the fuselage could be depressurised and that there could be a further possibility of an emergency landing at the nearest airfield if the fire could not be brought under control. The navigator quickly came up with distances and headings to Rome and was reading the emergency checks from the flight reference cards. The co-pilot took over flying the aircraft. I was busy switching off the radar, the feel simulator and the automatic pilot - all items that were situated at the front of the freight bay and could possibly be the source of the fire. The aircraft had to be slowed down to 200 knots to avoid overstressing the airframe, as this could easily happen now we were denied the use of the feel simulator. The flight engineer disappeared down through the hatch by the flight deck floor. I told the co-pilot to maintain his height until the nature and seriousness of the fire had been assessed.

After about four minutes the engineer re-appeared coughing and almost asphyxiated, to report that he could not find the cause of the fire mainly because the smoke was so dense down in the freight bay. What he did not tell me at the time was that he had to hack his way through the cargo net with an axe and that the tube on his smoke mask was too short to allow him to go right to the front of the hold to reach the probable cause of the fire. In fact he had been groping about in the smoke holding his breath and then dashing back to the smoke mask and/or the hatch for air.

I decided the situation was serious enough to start an emergency diversion to Rome. The engineer disappeared down into the

'One hundred passengers were asleep in the cabin and all was quiet.'

hold once more and this time he was assisted by the signaller. The density of the smoke seemed to be a little less on the flight deck, presumably because everything was switched off, and I could just make out the navigator's reassuring thumbs up as he bent over his table. Rome Control had by this time cleared the airway to accommodate our emergency.

As we passed 15,000 feet, the flight engineer reappeared and informed me that he thought the fire was in the feel simulator and that it was out. The smoke was clearing so we stopped our descent and cancelled our 'Mayday' (distress) call with Rome and requested permission to climb back and rejoin the airway to continue to the UK, albeit at a reduced airspeed because the feel simulator was switched off. I then switched on the cloud collision warning radar to check for cumulo-nimbus clouds ahead but once again all hell broke loose with more smoke and a further fire warning. It was now obvious to us what the cause was so the engineer quickly disappeared again with a fire extinguisher down to the freight bay and I quickly switched the cloud radar off. The smoke was thick on the flight deck again so it must have been unbearable in the hold. When the flight engineer finally re-emerged he was on the point of collapse. He was now able to assure me that it was the cloud collision warning radar on fire and that he had put it out with the extinguisher. He was coughing and pale with the amount of smoke inhalation he had endured.

With the feel simulator and autopilot back in use I could resume normal cruising speeds and heights. Fortunately there were no cumulo-nimbus clouds so the rest of the flight was uneventful and only a few of the passengers were aware that anything had been amiss.

In my report I praised my flight engineer's efforts and here is my actual report about his actions:

'The flight engineer's efforts were particularly praiseworthy. He is a big man and it was not easy for him to move about in the small space of the hatchway and amongst the freight. He had to cut away the cargo net, which had fouled the access hatch and then he found the

air tube was not long enough to allow him to reach the source of the fire so he had to keep returning to the mask or the hatchway for breath. He showed great tenacity and strength of character and he undoubtedly prevented a bad situation from getting worse.'

My flight engineer was subsequently recommended for the award of the Air Force Cross for his actions in this potentially serious emergency.

Chapter 17

THE SAGA OF THE RUNAWAY PROPELLER - DEC 1962

I have listed the names of the crew with their particular aircrew trade in this incident because the following is quoted from an article I wrote shortly after it happened in which I refer to crew members by their Christian names:

Roy	Co-pilot	Flight Lieutenant Johnson
George	Navigator	Flight Lieutenant Dobson
Bob	Flight Engineer	Master Engineer Anstee AFM
John	Signaller	Master Signaller Beardon AFM
Joe	Air Quartermaster	Sergeant Robinson
Phil	Shackleton	Flight Lieutenant Burton

It all really started in the Jungle Bar at RAF Khormaksar on the 12th December. Wing Commander John Lewis, OC 511 Squadron, was there at closing time and with his inimitable rallying call to his Squadron members of 'There'll be no trouble,' bought a bottle of Scotch and, of course, the party went on until the early morning!

Next morning I awoke with two pains, one was in my red and swollen little toe, which I thought was a bit odd, and the other in my head! Roy and George gave me unsympathetic looks and could throw no light on the cause. The Khormaksar Senior Medical Officer cheerfully told me I had broken it and so long as I rested it for 72 hours I would be fit to fly. The rest of my crew fell about laughing at my incapacity. I can only theorise that I had staggered to the 'loo' during the night in Merrifield House (the aircrew accommodation), pulled open the door and jammed it on to my toe.

We should have operated back to UK from Aden on 14th December but I was not going to be fit in time so HQ at RAF Upavon did some fast crew juggling and switched my crew with Geoff Shipway of 99 Squadron. Geoff and his merry men were on their way to Singapore to do their Christmas shopping so my crew and I were very unpopular indeed, in fact, vehemently so, as he and his crew became very disparaging about our parentage!

Therefore on 16th December 1962, we lumbered off the Khormaksar runway at thirty-six minutes past seven (Aden time) *en route* to Gan. The Flight Plan time was 6 hrs 30 mins with the usual forecast of cumulo-nimbus and associated weather across the Indian Ocean to Gan. We happily settled back at 15,500 feet in clear blue desert skies, crossed the east coast of the Horn of Africa and 'step-climbed' to 17,500 feet. Apart from only having clothes for a quick four-day 'slip' in winter at Aden, everything in the garden was lovely so far as we were concerned and we chattered about our unexpected good luck of a few days in Singapore. Bob, Roy and George cruelly exhorted me to break my toe more often! It still hurt a bit but so long as I did not press hard on the rudder pedals it did not bother me - little did I know what was to come!

I could hear frustrated curses behind me - John was surrounded in his usual blue haze of Woodbine cigarette smoke, his blue cloth helmet half pushed back on his head, clattering away on his Wireless Telegraphy key, sweating and swearing profusely about Bombay and Karachi operators who would not answer him. We passed our 'critical point' (i.e. exactly half way) uneventfully and just about four hours after take-off at 0715 Greenwich Mean Time, George laconically reported that we had just passed our 'Point of No Return'. Ten minutes later it happened!

I had earlier wandered down the back to have a chat and savour a cup of Joe's excellent tea. As I sat we noticed a slight aural beat creeping into the propeller synchronisation so I nipped forward to see what it was all about. I opened the flight deck door and prodded big Bob. He always tried to give the impression of being fierce but he was a great big softy really! He glowered at me and in his matter of fact way and growled, 'No.4 PRPM (propeller revolutions per minute) has crept up 15 rpm (revolutions) and I can't get the bloody thing back.' He turned back and continued to hypnotise the No.4 engine gauges. I leaned over behind Bob and peered at the instruments and was about to ask Roy a question but he gave me that withering look that comes over all co-pilot's faces from time to time which clearly says, 'When I've got everything under control, why do captains have to damn well interfere?' So I thought better of it and got back into my seat. As I strapped in Roy volunteered, 'We've tried toggling back on 'normal' and it looks as though it won't come back on 'standby' either.' After a few choice epithets from Bob he leaned back from the quadrant and shaking his head said, 'It's no good, captain; we've got a pitch-locked propeller.' I therefore told him to feather No.4, so Bob and Roy went through the feathering drill but nothing happened. They tried again but still no joy so I ordered them to carry out the feathering drill on the 'standby' system.

As they did so, all hell broke loose and a howl, rising in crescendo to an ear piercing scream, came from No.4 engine (right outer) as the 16 feet propeller broke loose from its reduction gear and oversped at a horrendous rate. The autopilot threw out and the aircraft yawed to the right. The No.4 rpm gauge needle slammed up against its stop and broke off! Thank God for the overspeed limiter, which cut the fuel and stopped the compressor or we definitely would not be here today. The compressor revolutions died away and No.4 oil pressure dropped back to zero. I yelled for 'flight idle' (closed throttles) and Bob slammed the throttles back so fast that the ultras (throttle electrical controls) latched out on number one and two throttles while number three shot back to flight idle. This meant that full power remained on the left wing with no power from the inner (No.3) engine plus enormous wind-milling drag from the outer one (No.4) on the right wing, and it was all trying to roll us to the right. I pulled the control column back to get the speed off quickly (to lessen the effect of the windmilling propeller) but with Nos.1 and 2 engines at maximum power I needed more than full left rudder. However, Bob quickly rectified Nos.1 and 2 ultra throttles and those two engines' power came back under control to idling. Nevertheless there was still a lot of drag from the No.4 windmilling propeller.

Once the speed was back to 120 knots the noise of No.4 propeller fell away, which meant we had reduced the wind-milling propeller's revolutions to a more acceptable level. We had no way of telling how much damage had been done or whether No.4 propeller would break off and crash into No.3 engine. I decided that if it did, our best chance in the event of massive structural damage would be down near the sea surface so that we could ditch instantly. Furthermore it would help to be below turbulent cumulous cloud so we began a tortuously slow descent at 120 knots. Turbulence created control problems initially and if the speed increased to as little as 140 knots vibration set in but we descended gradually.

I had already asked John to put out a 'Mayday' call, which he told me had been acknowledged - even by Karachi and Bombay! By now John was knee deep in fag ends and he peered round at me, his eyes bulging and bawled at me, 'For Christ's sake, Captain, NOT AGAIN!' Poor John, we had flown together for many years on the Overseas Ferry Unit and had crewed up on the Britannia but almost every time we got airborne together something went wrong! We had forced landed in the desert in an Anson (Ch.9), nearly incinerated ourselves in a Lancaster (Ch.9) over the Mediterranean and frightened ourselves in a Shackleton. John transfixed me with a somewhat plaintiff look and added, 'You are bloody bad news to fly with!' In these sorts of circumstances he had to depend on me to save his life but we had always pulled through in the past and hopefully we would again!

Roy was working like a 'one-armed paper hanger'. He had depressurised, transferred and balanced the fuel and was passing fuel flows to George as often as possible as well as helping me to fly the lumbering and wallowing great beast. Bob was dashing to and fro trying to assess any damage or signs of fire out on No.4 engine and helped Joe to lash and secure the freight in case of emergency ditching. Joe briefed his passengers and prepared them for ditching. In fact the crew had all clicked into the many and necessary emergency drills like a well-oiled machine. We donned our life jackets and rehearsed our ditching drills. Our painstakingly disciplined and thorough RAF training in the classroom and the constantly practised emergency drills in the simulator now more than paid off. I told John to tell our HQ at Upavon the symptoms and details of our emergency in case we perished so that the engineers back at base would know what had happened and prevent a possible re-occurrence.

By the time we reached the surface of the sea everything we could think of had been done. Bob reopened the No.4 oil cock, which had been closed during the feathering drill but we noticed it was emptying quite fast. This presented a monumental problem since it probably meant there was a leak and the wind-milling propeller was being starved of oil so it might just be a matter of time before the reduction gear became molten metal. I instructed Bob to open the cock for 30 seconds every 10 minutes and we simply prayed enough oil was hopefully somehow reaching the engine. What we did not know at that time was that the fire extinguisher system to No.4 had also been severed and was useless. Just as well we did not know perhaps!

We took stock of our situation. On the plus side John came up with the good news that Gan, Aden, Karachi and Bombay had acknowledged our 'MAYDAY' and knew our exact position. All emergency services had been alerted, shipping in the area was listening out on 500kcs, (the international distress frequency), and were altering course towards our intended track. But best news of all was that the Air Sea Rescue Shackleton was being scrambled from Gan and an ASR launch had set course on our reciprocal track to meet us, plus the helicopter at Gan was standing by. Good reliable John, always at his most dependable in adversity, had more that done his stuff.

Without pressurisation and air conditioning the greenhouse effect on the flight deck down at sea level made the temperature and humidity rise so we all sat like dehydrated grease pots. Joe poured fluid down our throats as fast as he could - he constantly appeared from down the back with a smile on his face and a cheery word almost as if nothing had happened.

Just as the tension started to subside George dropped his bombshell! Without any emotion in his voice he laconically announced, 'Captain, we haven't got enough fuel to get to Gan!' You could have heard a pin drop. Charming! As if our troubles weren't enough, we now had a certain ditching to look forward to (a Britannia had never been successfully ditched before). George sarcastically reckoned that on present fuel flows it was about 4 hours to ditching and 4½ hrs to Gan! If we went higher to reduce fuel consumption the propeller rpm and vibration would increase and we would be in turbulent cloud. There was still the overriding problem of the need to ditch the aircraft as quickly as possible if the propeller came off and caused irreparable damage. Catch 22! Anyway, we eased up to 1500 feet just below the cloud base and decided to sweat it out. At least if we ditched with empty tanks the aircraft might float for a while!

George was unflappable. Throughout the whole emergency he remained extremely cool. His low-level navigation was superb. He kept John supplied with updated and (as it turned out) very accurate positions and with Roy's assistance he continuously monitored and calculated our fuel situation. Apart from an occasional nervous glance through his window at the offending propeller, he bent over his charts in his usual quiet and efficient manner.

Roy was a tremendous help to me. My wretched toe had begun to make its presence felt so he helped me fly the lumbering beast between standing in for Bob (who kept dashing down the back) and continuously passing fuel flows to George. We tried the autopilot with only partial success - it did not like the amount of rudder needed to counteract the drag caused by the windmilling propeller at such a low airspeed and threw out regularly, but it was some help. Roy was of the Roman Catholic faith and he kept religiously crossing himself as he frantically transmitted on the two pilot-operated emergency frequencies, (there was another Britannia about 40 minutes ahead of us) without a reply. Bob grinned at him and at one point and said sarcastically, 'Co-pilot, he's obviously busy and not listening out on your frequencies!'

I heard a cheer ago up from behind me as John joyfully shouted that the ASR Shackleton was airborne. Seemingly it had been on a Minor Star Servicing (i.e. in bits!) when our SOS had come in at Gan. The ground crews had pitched in and helped to slap it all together, which they had achieved, miraculously, in just 55 minutes - a magnificent effort in such a short time.

After about another hour we had another piece of cheering news. George quietly announced that on his latest fuel calculations we might just make Gan. We had earlier considered jettisoning the freight but unfortunately most of it was too large to get through the rear door (Sea Slug missiles all crated up), and Bob and Joe had decided there was a risk of the smaller stuff striking the tail plane because of our very high nose-up attitude.

In a superb display of skill and airmanship the Shackleton, captained by Flt Lt Phil Burton, intercepted us 320 nautical miles from Gan at 1013 GMT. It wheeled round and formated on our starboard wing tip. Our reaction was that of pride and joy to see the big dark grey Shackleton with Phil waving to us through his open side window. It did our morale a world of good - it was a sight none of us will ever forget.

It was not all over yet despite our friendly Shackleton alongside. We still had about two hours to go. Our hearts began to sink when about one hour from Gan the vibration started to increase alarmingly. I told Bob to increase the ration of oil to No.4 engine despite the fact that the gauge was now showing nearly empty, but it did not help and the oil ran out about 25 miles from Gan.

We got ready to ditch but at long last we saw Gan Island on the horizon, (George had done a magnificent job of navigating), with the fuel gauges reading zero. We were so near yet so far! With hearts in mouths and fingers crossed, we slowly drew nearer.

We spotted the wake of the Air Sea Rescue (ASR) launch speeding towards us and we were told the ASR 'chopper' (helicopter) was airborne - just in time, as the vibration was getting worse. The weather was with us, thank God, (I think Roy had got through to 'Him' somehow after all), with the wind down the runway from the east and the sun setting behind us. We did our checks and prayed and our hearts did not stop pounding till our wheels touched the runway after those nine hours in the air.

We taxied in and shut down with a sigh of relief. A corporal went beneath No.4 engine to undo the cowlings and as he did so the sheer weight of the mangled engine parts forced open the lower cowling doors and gashed his head. He was lucky to escape worse injury as the remains of the reduction gear then crashed to the tarmac narrowly missing him.

Wing Commander Peter Ellis, the Station Commander, and the Officer Commanding designate, Wing Commander P G Hill, followed by most of Gan servicing personnel, bounded up the steps to see if we were OK. The Station Commander had very thoughtfully produced a crate of ice-cold Tiger Beer so we sat on the aircraft steps, thoroughly dehydrated but exhilarated and relieved at our escape. We watched as Phil brought his dark grey Shackleton low across the pan in salute. My toe hurt like hell (I had not noticed it until now!) It was the BEST beer we had EVER tasted making it an extremely nice ending to a very long traumatic day, a day that has been etched in our memories ever since. It made us very emotional and near to tears to think of the magnificent response from everyone at Gan.

Back in the UK there was much disharmony between the RAF engineering staff and the aircraft manufacturers about the cause of this most serious incident; so much so that at one point Don Stoneham, our propeller expert at Lyneham, walked out of a meeting when the makers accused the RAF of mishandling the aircraft. We, as the crew, can only plead 'NOT GUILTY'!'

Chapter 18

SOME WEATHER HAZARDS OF THE INDIAN OCEAN

Some flights across the Indian Ocean from Malaya to Gan can be uneventful but when the Intercontinental Convergence Zone (ITCZ) lies along the track the 6½-hour flight can be hazardous. The ITCZ is where two air masses mix, the southwest monsoon meets the northeast monsoon, giving rise to massive and very active cloud formations with imbedded extremely active thunderstorms.

The night of August 30th was black - the forecast for the leg from Gan to Changi was not good. I took off in clear weather from Gan and settled down at my cruising height of 13,000 feet. Everything seemed fine; the radar was working perfectly, as were the engines and instruments. I was due to arrive at Changi just after dawn. Several hours later the navigator reported weather on the radar at 120 miles range but this was nothing new or anything to worry about when crossing the Bay of Bengal - it was routine to have to battle through the weather in that part of the world.

The higher-flying jets have little trouble but the poor old Britannia's operating heights in the tropics coincided with the icing temperatures for the Britannia's Proteus engine between +2°C to +12°C air temperature. (Engine icing becomes particularly bad between +2°C and +6°C). Ice builds up in the engine intakes and lumps break off and become ingested in the engine sufficient to put the flame out. The engine was designed to overcome this hazard with a device called a 'glow plug', which re-ignites the flame but not without a bang, called 'engine bumping'. If the icing is particularly bad the ice lumps can flame out the engine altogether and should this happen the hapless crew have to jump to it and carry out the 'rapid relight' drill. If it happens continuously on all four engines it is a nerve-racking operation relighting each engine one after the other, involving all the flight deck crew.

The obvious way to avoid this hazard is to fly outside the really dangerous icing range (+2°C to + 6°C indicated outside air temp. (IOAT)), but this is only possible where sufficient fuel is available to fly at much lower (and warmer) altitudes initially, and then climb to much higher (colder) altitudes - but this means the aircraft must have burned off sufficient fuel to be light enough to climb up to a higher designated flight level. The normal pattern of operating the Britannia in the tropics was, therefore, what was known as 'low/high' cruise. Take on a little extra fuel to accommodate flying low (around 11,000 to 13,000 feet) to remain above (higher than) the +6 °C IOAT icing limit. When sufficient weight of fuel is burned off, climb as fast as possible through the +6°C to + 2°C band to cruise at a temperature below (lower than) +2°C indicated outside air temperature (usually around 19,000 to 21,000 feet).

My navigator had calculated his fuel requirement to Singapore based on a forecast tailwind but, as so often happened in that part of the world, the tail wind turned out to be a headwind, which meant we would have to fly higher to conserve fuel. We were too heavy at that stage to climb above the icing range so we settled down at 17,000 feet and as soon as weight would allow we would climb further. We were soon flying in medium cloud. It is a feature of flying into cloud that the indicated 'indicated outside air temperature' (IOAT) drops as the aircraft enters the cloud. The co-pilot reported the IOAT to be +13°C and as we entered the cloud the IOAT rapidly fell to +10°C. Engine anti-icing controls were immediately switched on and all went well for about an hour until the cumulus and cumulonimbus clouds became so numerous it was difficult to weave around them even with the help of the radar. At this stage it became necessary to reduce speed to the 'turbulence penetration speed'.

'... until the cumulus and cumulo-nimbus clouds became so numerous it was difficult to weave around them ...'

We were in a 'Hobson's Choice' situation. Passengers were warned and they were all strapped in tight. The blackness of the flight deck was only broken by the glow of the instruments at the front and the navigator's gentle light behind. His continuous patter guided us between the bright lightning flashes and more turbulent storms. I had disengaged the automatic pilot, which must not be used in turbulence, so the co-pilot and I took turns to keep the aircraft on an even keel. The reduced speed in turn lowered the IOAT and the much thicker clouds meant increased water content, which further reduced the IOAT. (Inside cumulo-nimbus clouds rain is falling from much higher altitudes and is consequently much colder). The occasional engine 'bump' now became frequent ones but so far we had not had a full flameout.

It was getting to the stage when we must go up higher to get out of the icing and to conserve fuel. The trouble is that if the aircraft is too heavy there is a point where it reaches a near zero rate of climb and if this is within the dangerous icing range we would be in serious trouble. Fortunately the Britannia ODMs (Operating Data Manual) are provided to tell whether or not the height can be achieved. I opted to go up a little earlier than the 'book' recommended because continuous operation at 200 knots (turbulence penetration speed) was well below the normal cruising speed for the operating altitude using up precious fuel reserves. Once at a higher altitude the engines would be operating at maximum continuous power (MCP) and therefore at maximum efficiency. (Jet engines, even turboprops, are more efficient at higher altitudes.) I increased power to MCP (Maximum Continuous Power) and we started to climb.

The co-pilot and engineer stood by to re-light the engines as the IOAT gradually dropped below +6°C. The 'bumping' continued unabated and at +2°C we had a couple of flame-outs but the drill was so well practised in the simulator back at Lyneham that it seemed little different to the real thing. The last 500 feet of the climb was as little as 100 feet per minute but, at long last, we were able to level the aircraft and wait for the speed to build up. However, the cruise speed was below what it should have been according to the 'book' because the aircraft was a bit too heavy through climbing too early.

Not long after we levelled off the words every Britannia captain dreads crackled over the intercom, 'Captain, the radar's packed in and I can't fix it,' the navigator intoned! It meant we were now blind. The Cloud Collision Warning Radar (CCWR) 'sees' cloud on its screen as white blobs and violent turbulence centres as black 'holes' in the middle. The bigger the 'hole', the more violent the up and down currents. There was no moon, it was pitch black and we were in thick altostratus cloud. I warned the passengers over the public address system to ensure they had still got their lap straps tight. I prayed we would not run into a really bad one. As the aircraft ran into thicker lumps of cloud, the noise level increased as larger raindrops hammered on the fuselage and windscreen. At least we did not now have the added hazard of the engine icing to worry about. Just before we entered the turbulence of a thunderstorm the rain started to turn to hail and the aircraft was caught in a violent lurch and the hail smashed against us.

At one point a blinding flash of lightning struck the nose of the aeroplane with a loud bang. Our hearts missed a beat in case it had made a hole in the fuselage and explosive decompression might follow but nothing untoward happened apart from the two compasses giving a twirl. (We found a small dent in the nose after we landed).

An hour and a quarter later the turbulence eased slowly and then quite suddenly we emerged into clear inky blue sky with stars twinkling and far away on the horizon to the east the reddish grey hue of the dawn greeted us. We sat back in our seats and heaved sighs of relief. I felt quite drained and exhausted, as did the rest of the crew. It is a stressful ordeal to fly through the ITCZ at night without radar. The massive thunderstorms of the tropics can reach as high as 60,000 feet so even the modern high flying jet airliner (with exception of Concorde!) cannot escape the weather altogether. But, without doubt, the up and down draughts in these storms are at their very worst between 15,000 and 25,000 feet.

The corporal steward appeared through the flight deck door with a strong cup of coffee each. He reported that most of the passengers had been sick - it is far worse down the back not knowing what is going on. He looked a little pale and strained himself. After another hour the sun peeped over the eastern horizon and started to glare through the front windscreen. At that time of the morning, after being up all night, I always felt I had sand in my eyes and my mouth tasted like a 'Japanese wrestlers jock-strap'. It was just another one of those nights just slightly more than routine but part of the life of a

Long Range Transport pilot (a 'Truckie'). (Transport Command pilots were rudely referred to as 'Truck Drivers', which gave rise to the slang word 'Truckie'!)

We passed over Sumatra bathed in slanting morning sunlight and turned right at the coast of Malaya and on down the Straits of Sumatra. That part of the world always looked the same at dawn with the blankets of fog shrouding the valleys and the deep green jungle peeping up through. Soon Singapore Island came in sight with the friendly voice of the Chinese controller issuing routing instructions to Changi. As the Britannia dropped down into the hot humid atmosphere of Singapore, mist started to form on the windscreen and condensation dripped copiously from the cold metal of the interior of the flight deck on to our uniforms. The temperature on board slowly started to rise from the pleasant coolness of higher up. By the time we touched down on Changi runway (the humidity at dawn was always at its highest), we were all running with perspiration and looking forward to a few ice-cold Tiger Beers and having a good sleep. To many a tired transport crew that final 'wind-down' beer was a beneficial relaxation at any time of the night or day, and made the concentration and trials and tribulations seem worthwhile.

Chapter 19

THE ROYAL MALAYASIAN AIR FORCE 1963 - 66
(TENTERA UDARA DI-RAJA MALAYSIA)

In 1963 the Ministry of Defence asked for volunteers to be seconded to the Royal Malaysian Air Force (RMAF) to introduce the new Handley Page Herald. The requirements asked were for pilots who had turbo-prop and transport pilot experience, but the plum job was the Flight Commander's post, a situation that demanded a Qualified Flying Instructor as well as an above average captain on turbo-prop transport aircraft i.e. the Britannia.

I volunteered and was overjoyed to hear that not only had I been selected but also for the Flight Commander post, because normally it would only go to a 'Career Officer'. (I was commissioned from the ranks in 1954 and was granted a 'Branch Commission', which at that time meant full time flying but very limited promotion prospects, i.e. not a 'career' commission. Later, commissions of this kind became known as 'Specialist Aircrew' which also restricted their career to flying aeroplanes and promotion limited to the rank of Squadron Leader).

Initially I went to Rolls Royce at Derby for a week's course on the Dart turbo-prop engine. This was followed by two weeks ground instruction on the Herald at the Handley Page factory at Radlett. But a shortage of Heralds at the factory, including the non-appearance of my

Handley Page Herald.

own Malaysian Herald, necessitated me going to Jersey to have my flying conversion with Jersey Airlines on one of their Heralds. I spent eight very pleasant days in a Jersey hotel at the expense of Handley Page!

I returned to Radlett to find my aircraft being painted and soon ready for flight testing. I was able to watch the final completion work each day and made suggestions for minor user orientated modifications to the cockpit from civilian to military use. I eventually left Radlett in the first Herald, on 2nd November 1963, destined for Malaysia. The aircraft was painted in a smart blue and white livery, with the words *'Tenera Udara Di-Raja Malaysia'* on the fuselage, which when translated, means 'The Royal Malaysian Air Force'. Since the aircraft did not have long-range tanks, each leg was comparatively short with quick refuels. So I night stopped at Naples, Nicosia, Bahrain, Karachi, and Calcutta - quite an interesting itinerary and I landed at Kuala Lumpur exactly on schedule to be greeted by the Chief of the Air Staff of the Royal Malaysian Air Force.

This brand new aircraft straight out of the factory did not have any unserviceability all the way out. I found the Herald was one of the most serviceable, pleasant and reliable transport aircraft I have ever flown.

Yet again I was forced to leave my family behind but my wife flew out to join me on a civil aircraft to Singapore about three months later. The Malaysians were very understanding when she did arrive and allowed me to take a Heron down to RAF Changi to collect her and bring her up to Kuala Lumpur.

RMAF Heron.

My two children were now in boarding school and came out to Malaysia twice a year at the RAF's expense. We lived in a very nice bungalow in nearby Petaling Jaya for about a year then moved into a Married Quarter on the RMAF Base Sempang in Kuala Lumpur. Our life was very pleasant indeed with plenty of socialising with the Malaysians as well as the 'secondees'. KL was a fine city with great shopping facilities. Dorothy, my wife, got a job and learned to drive and was quite happy.

In the meantime, until she arrived, I 'lived in' at the Malaysian Officers' Mess, which was a bit bare with no inducement to work in my room. The Mess at that time had not yet started to cater for European food either! My health suffered a bit and I found it hard going until Dorothy arrived and I was able to move out of the Mess and eat well again!

The RMAF had a small training element, which was being built up, but all of the instructors were seconded. With the addition of East Malaysia (Borneo) to the Federation, the long lines of communication over the sea made it necessary to have a transport aircraft capable of carrying troops and freight over the distances involved. The Malaysians had no indigenous pilots experienced enough to fly the new Heralds so pilots were recruited from the UK and Australasia.

The Herald squadron was formed as No.4 Squadron and initially four aircraft were ferried out, followed by another four a year later. If I had been doing my current job as Flight Commander and Training Officer on a RAF squadron, I would have had the backing of the Aeroplane & Armament Experimental Establishment (A&AEE). They would have already carried out the trials and tests to lay down guidelines, written the Pilot's Notes and advised on how to operate the aeroplane under training and operational conditions. This had not been done on the military Herald so I was obliged to do it, to the best of my ability

However, in this case, although the Herald was operated as a civilian aircraft, it had never been used before in a military capacity. The RMAF Heralds differed from civilian aircraft by having strengthened freight floors, roller conveyors, freight doors and paratroop dropping capability etc. It was very flexible and capable of being converted, in a short time, from carrying 50 passengers in comfortable seats to a complete freighter role or half and half. It could also be used in the aero medical role with stretchers, or even in a VIP role with a very plush interior. (The King and Queen of Malaysia and the Prime Minister often used it in this role).

The actual military performance of the aircraft had yet to be proved and data books had to be written to cover all its operational tasks. Pilot's Notes, as military pilots understand them, had to be written and printed. Flight Reference Cards had to be designed and written out; standard operating procedures had to be tried and written up.

Short field performances, parachute dropping trials and proving flights to all the airfields in Malaya and Borneo had to be tried out and tested. Emergency drills had to be thoroughly checked to ensure standardisation of techniques. Pilots had to have all their emergency procedures drilled into them on the ground and in the air before they could be permitted to carry passengers. No such situation had existed before as there had not been a medium sized transport aircraft in this emergent little air force before. It looked as though I was going to be very busy!

Shortly after my arrival I was horrified to find out that no one in the RMAF Headquarters Planning Staff had appreciated that it was necessary to have a loadmaster to supervise passengers in flight, load the Heralds, and supervise emergency drills to vacate the passengers in the event of ditching or crash-landing. Hastily recruited Malay,

Cessna 310F, Royal Malaysian Air Force.

Chinese and Indian airmen who had not got a clue about the job, and never flown before, had to be trained as loadmasters. In some cases, they could not understand or speak English to the required standard. (This proved a Herculean task!). Later the loadmasters-to-be were sent to the UK to be trained, thank God! I even had to design and produce a weight and balance sheet for loading Heralds. If too much weight is put too far forward or too far aft, the aircraft could become unstable and crash after take-off; so balance is an extremely important factor in loading aeroplanes. Similarly, it is easy to put too much weight in the fuselage so that the aeroplane is overloaded and would not be able to take off from some of the smaller strips in Borneo from which they were called upon to operate.

    I found myself working up to 18 hours every day flying, training and lecturing, designing and writing operating manuals etc. In those early days I wondered many times what I had let myself in for but I enjoyed the challenge and loved the kind of work it involved. I got great job satisfaction from it. On the many first flights into Borneo, before I had trained our loadmasters, my co-pilot and I had to stand at the rear door loading the aircraft ourselves, taking soldier's kit and guessing the weight - saying, 'That's about 25 pounds,'

Another shot of a RMAF Herald.

and then looking at the soldier and saying, 'He's about 140 pounds!' Very often Malaysian soldiers would come to the aircraft straight from the jungle with baby pythons or pet orang utangs clinging round their necks (and monkeys can be airsick we found out and pythons were forbidden!) It was a very primitive little 'airline' but it worked!

    The Squadron had some seconded RAF SNCO technicians as a backbone but the rest of the squadron consisted of Malaysian airmen of Malay, Chinese and Indian races and they all had to be trained. The CO was therefore content to leave the operational flying organisation and training to me while he battled with the very complex Malaysian airmen's training and administration! One of his biggest problems was the 'loss of face' complex, whereby indigenous airmen on the Squadron would not admit to any technical error on their part because of 'loss of face'!

    All the most senior officers from the Chief of the Air Staff down were from the RAF and most of the pilots at that time were of European race. I think facts speak for themselves when one looks at today's Royal Malaysian Air Force. It is a very efficient organisation and now operates some very sophisticated aeroplanes. It reflects great credit on those early-seconded pioneers who built up with fortitude, guts and sheer hard work, the foundations of that new air force through 'Malaysianisation' and turned it into what it is today.

    With few exceptions, the Malaysians accepted the fact that

Europeans staffed their Air Force and relations were extremely good. The population of Malaysia consists of Malays (the indigenous race), Chinese and Indians. I found them all to be polite, kindly and charming people. We seconded personnel all wore RMAF uniform (green khaki drill) with Malaysian pilot's wings, blue stockings and a songkok worn on the head. (The songkok was a bit like a pillbox with the RMAF hat badge). Ranks were the same as those used by the Royal Air Force.

The first indigenous Malaysian came to No.4 Squadron in April 1964, a Chinese Flying Officer known as 'Danny'. An Indian named Maniam followed and he was nicknamed 'Wilf', much to his amusement when it was explained to him who Wilf Maniam was! Both progressed to become captains in the left seat and Manian eventually became a 747 Jumbo captain with Singapore Airways.

In 1964 Indonesian troops made landings on Malaysian territory and managed to infiltrate into the jungle and President Sukarno of Indonesia made trouble around the Malay Peninsular. He even withdrew his country from the United Nations in January 1965

RMAF uniform- green with blue socks! Songkok hat.

155

and the whole of the Far East was then in turmoil.

Thus 'Confrontation' (the war between Malaysia and Indonesia) had begun in earnest. By now the Herald squadron was fully operational and geared for war. Training had advanced to the extent that many Malaysians had progressed to qualify as co-pilots.

Chapter 20
THE HERALD AT WAR
1963 - 66

The Malaysianisation of the RMAF began to take on slightly less importance when the war with Indonesia began. The operational tasks for the Heralds poured in and very soon regular scheduled flights three times per week to East Malaysia were instituted. In these, and in all its tasks, the Herald proved utterly reliable, so much so that the RAF in Singapore and Borneo were able to set their watches by its regularity and timekeeping. The Herald could carry 50 fully armed troops or 10,000lbs of freight to Kuching, Labuan, Sandakan or Tawau. The height of the freight door was such that a three-ton army truck could be reversed up to it and the tailgate of the truck was exactly the same height as the sill, so that boxes of freight could be slid straight on board. As an operational aircraft it was worth its weight in gold and became a massive contribution to the air war of 'Confrontation', as well as the many and varied other tasks No.4 Squadron undertook throughout the war.

At the very start of Confrontation, in December, a patrol of Malay soldiers was attacked by the Indonesians in the jungle of Khear Kalmaton in Borneo and eight of them were killed. This was a most serious event and the nation was shocked. The Prime Minister, Tunku Abdul Rahman, personally ordered a Herald to fetch the bodies back. The bodies had been carried out of the jungle to Tawau and by the time they were loaded onto the Herald they had been dead for over 72 hours. They were laid out on stretchers in the aircraft covered only with bloodstained sheets; in the tropical heat they were beginning to decompose. The stench in the aircraft was indescribable so I had the poor loadmaster come and remain on the flight deck and kept the crew door firmly closed.

I made the mistake of opening a clear vision panel on the side of the windscreen to try to ventilate the aircraft as soon as it was depressurised on the descent but this sucked all the foul air from the rear of the aircraft into the cockpit and made us nearly vomit on the approach into Sempang airfield at Kuala Lumpur! The Prime Minister and many of the nation's religious leaders were at the aircraft steps to welcome home the emergent nation's first dead heroes. After this incident, I insisted that the bodies were sealed in body bags before air transporting them home.

Later on there was an amusing incident resulting from this - I had taken off from Tawau with a body, this time in a sealed foil bag inside a cardboard coffin. Half way up the climb to cruising altitude the Indian loadmaster appeared at my elbow, his face contorted with fear and in a very agitated state. He shouted, 'The body is trying to get out, captain!' What was happening was that as the aircraft

Line-up at Alor Star with the Prime Minister of Malaysia, Tunku Abdul Rahman. (At the left Sgt Sayid (Chapter 23) and 2nd right Fg Off Brian Love).

climbed, the pressure in the cabin decreased, but as the metal foil round the body was sealed, the pressure inside remained at ground level and was expanding the metal foil making strange creaking and knocking noises! The demented loadmaster, who was not convinced, would not go near the coffin for the rest of the flight! He was not alone as all the Malaysian soldiers on board were peering at the coffin with terror on their faces, especially as the noises began again as the aircraft descended!

In February I flew the Prime Minister, Tunku Abdul Rahman, to Phnom Penh to meet Prince Sihanouk, the ruler of Cambodia. My co-pilot and I were treated as part of the official party and even attended the welcoming banquet in the evening. The next day we all went to Siem Reap in two Ilyushin 14s (very much like a Dakota). At Siem Reap there was an awful plague of flying creatures like enormous cockroaches and they swarmed everywhere in their thousands but particularly attracted to lights at night. Many crawled around on the ground and as I walked some were sickeningly crunched underfoot.

We accompanied the Tunku to the temple ruins at Angkor Watt, the site of an ancient civilisation, to witness a performance of a type of Cambodian opera. The actors and dancers had spotlights on them and the flying cockroaches were there also, swarming all over the players and audience in their thousands, in their hair, on their clothes and crawling all over us as well - it was quite revolting! My crew and I were very well looked after and were wined and dined at the best hotel and taken to see the sights of Phnom Penh. The Cambodian Air Force was also most hospitable to us for the five days we spent there.

The Herald was now gradually being used more and more for VIP flights. It had a very plush VIP fit, as mentioned before, that could be installed quite quickly. As yet I was the only VIP qualified pilot on the squadron so I was called upon more and more as Government Ministers realised that it vastly increased their status symbol by arriving at their destination in a gleaming blue and white Malaysian Air Force Herald! In the Herald the VIPs also found they could fly in pressurised comfort above the weather, quickly and directly, and were able to consume alcohol in flight, (which was actually against their religion!). I thoroughly enjoyed this type of flying.

Trials were carried out to re-supply the many small 'forts' scattered over the Malay Peninsular. These proved tricky, and required skilful handling as the forts were situated in valleys between mountains. The approaches to most of these forts needed a full flap dive at 115-120 knots into the valley, followed by a quick reduction down to dropping speed of 80 knots to get the supplies out, then full power to climb out of the valley. But it was considered risky in the event of an engine failure unless the valley was wide enough to allow a steep turn on one engine to permit an escape route back out. In fact this never actually happened as the Rolls Royce Dart engine was one of the most reliable engines made at that time. I thoroughly enjoyed this aspect of the operational use of the Herald and I gradually trained up the rest of the pilots.

The pace of flying increased rapidly as the Squadron slowly built up to full strength of eight aircraft. The operational tasks with the war in Borneo became the priority together with the scheduled services to maintain communications and supplies to the troops fighting there. With the commitment to the policy of Malaysianisation, (i.e. training up the indigenous pilots and the intense supply dropping training), I found myself often exceeding 100 hours flying each month, which, in that hot and humid climate I found a bit exhausting.

Operating the Herald in Borneo often involved the use of small strips for landing and as the war progressed it called for a great amount of versatility and improvisation from the crews. There was no ground assistance at many of the far flung little runways, hacked out of the jungle, where we landed. This meant that the captain, co-pilot and loadmaster would have to unload and load the aircraft ourselves just as we did in the early days. The Malay soldier passengers still often appeared like termites from the jungle, filthy and wet, the odd one with a baby orang-utan clinging to them. As mentioned before, the weight of the soldiers and their luggage had to be guessed at. It says much for the Herald that there was never any problem with weight and balance or its ability to take-off fully loaded from those short runways. It was rough and ready but it worked and there was never an accident.

Chapter 21

A ROYAL FLIGHT AND A MEDIVAC

In July, I had just completed a full day of operations around Borneo and landed at Jesselton (now called Kota Kinabalu) for a good night's rest. Just before I picked up my first pint of beer in the Flying Club I was informed that a Malay soldier had very serious head wounds and would die unless he was rushed to a hospital in Kuala Lumpur for a specialist operation - and would I fly him there!

I immediately agreed to fly the poor man if a stretcher and doctor could be found to accompany him. However, many of the items needed to sustain the man's life during the

In conversation with the Prime Minister.

161

Air Commodore Alasdair Steedman inspecting No.4 Squadron at Kuala Lumpar. He remarked about the lady in the nude behind him! At right is an Australian secondee; left is the CO of the Squadron, Sqn Ldr 'Buggie' Bryan.

flight could not be found at Jesselton so it was decided to take a massive gamble and airlift him initially to Labuan, ten minutes away, where RAF aero medical facilities existed. It was a very necessary risk to take to fly him to Labuan just on a stretcher but I hoped his life might be saved by doing so.

Due to his critical condition it was very quickly arranged that the correct airborne installation stretcher, plasma, oxygen equipment and a doctor with the necessary medical knowledge of head injuries would be kindly supplied by the RAF at Labuan.

Night flying facilities did not exist at RAF Labuan but when they were informed of the nature of the life or death emergency they hastily put out 'goose neck' paraffin lamps and the Medical Centre organised everything needed for the onward flight to Kuala Lumpur. I then flew him through the night to land at dawn in Kuala Lumpur and it was only then that I was able to make contact with my HQ to let them know I was on my way!

I was told later that he (his name was Private Mohammed Ali!) survived and that his life had been saved. I received a personal thankyou from the Prime Minister and the following one from the Chief of the Air Staff:

Dear Norman,

I have received a letter from Major General Hamid, Chief of the General Staff, expressing his appreciation for the prompt action on your part, which, it would seem, saved the life of a soldier. I have now been acquainted with the full facts of the steps you took to bring the badly wounded soldier back to Kuala Lumpur. Clearly you showed the most commendable initiative and, in so doing, brought great credit on yourself and your crew. It is probably not necessary for me to add that your action has also enhanced the prestige of No.4 Squadron and the Royal Malaysian Air Force. Very well done indeed

Yours sincerely

J West

Air Commodore
Chief of the Air Staff,
Royal Malaysian Air Force.

      Perhaps my most memorable flight was a Royal Flight taking the King and Queen of Malaysia on a seven-day tour of East Malaysia (Borneo). The Queen took a keen interest in the flying and spent a lot of her time on the flight deck. The King of Malaysia (translated) is 'Yang Di Pertuan Agong'; so the vehicle allotted to us at one place we visited had a highly visible notice in Malay saying 'King's Pilot'! No one dared to stop my co-pilot, my Malay loadmaster (who couldn't get over it!) or myself while we were there!
      The Royal Air Force provided a fighter escort in the form of two Javelins because the 'Confrontation' war meant that Indonesia was taking an unhealthy interest in the Royal Aircraft! We were treated like royalty, (excuse the pun!), and went everywhere with the royal party to all the banquets, receptions, displays and parades and we had a wonderful insight of Malay culture and overall had a most enjoyable seven days.
      As it was my first Royal Flight I appreciated it as a great

The 'Royal' crew at Jessleton, 1966.

honour, being allowed to fly the King and Queen of Malaysia. Not many foreign nationals are trusted with the lives of another nation's King and Queen.

On another occasion, three senior Conservative MPs, who were on their way to Kuala Lumpur as guests of the Tunku, the Prime Minister of Malaysia, were stranded in Singapore when their chartered civil aircraft became unserviceable. The Tunku 'phoned the Squadron and within an hour I was on my way to pick up Edward Heath, Chris Chataway and Paul Barber. Two days later I flew them up to Vietnam.

At Saigon Airport we were held off in the air while USAF aircraft took off for a bombing mission over Vietnam. Once on the ground I was given directions to the wrong dispersal so there was no VIP welcoming party there! The disappointed and upset Edward Heath then came forward to the flight deck in a filthy tantrum and tried to blame me! Eventually the welcoming party came racing from wherever they originally were and escorted the three away.

Chapter 22

AVM 'JOHNNIE' JOHNSON AND A BASSET HOUND

When the first four Heralds were purchased by the RMAF they did not have automatic pilots. For a while we flew them to and fro and around East Malaysia without auto pilots but we found it too tiring so it was decided to ferry them back to the UK one by one to have them fitted. I ferried one back with Flying Officer Brian Love, (who incidentally, many years later, was the First Officer on the aircraft that caught fire on the runway at Manchester with the loss of many lives), and two of our seconded SNCO engineers from our squadron.

On the way to the UK we routed through Baghdad, (this was prior to Saddam Hussein's time), but through some poor administration our diplomatic clearances had gone astray. When we landed at Baghdad we were put under close arrest because the Iraqis were suspicious of a strange Malaysian aircraft arriving unannounced flown by two pale faced pilots with British passports! Because it was a weekend no one could be contacted at the Malaysian Consulate or the British Embassy. Fortunately a helpful BOAC station manager rescued us in the nick of time by contacting Kuala Lumpur on his teleprinter only minutes before we were about to be thrown into an Iraqi gaol!

As a result of that incident we decided to give Baghdad a miss on the way back and went via Aden and thence to Delhi. When we landed at Aden a Wing Commander, whose name I have forgotten, asked me if I would do a 'favour' for the AOC Middle East, Air Vice Marshal 'Johnnie' Johnson, and take a beagle basset hound to Delhi in my aircraft. I agreed after a lengthy discussion about security, paper work and clearances etc. It appeared that the AVM wanted to take the dog, called 'Desmond', to Delhi himself in his own Argosy aircraft but the Ministry of Defence had vetoed it. He had arranged for the dog's transfer from the Royal Hunt in UK and it had been flown out to him in a Hastings to Aden. The dog was to be a personal gift from the AVM to the Royal Delhi Hunt. In the meantime the AVM was looking after Desmond at his residence in Aden until it could be taken to Delhi, and the two of them had become quite attached to one another. My Herald transiting through Aden presented itself as a Godsend and a very convenient way to get Desmond to Delhi after all!

At the time Johnnie Johnson was at Masirah on an inspection in his Argosy, (after which it was his original (vetoed) plan to go on to Delhi). I was told that 'Johnnie' would be there at Masirah to welcome Desmond when I transited through. He was, indeed, waiting at the steps with his entourage. My two Sergeant engineers let the dog out down the steps for his VIP welcome, but much to the AVM's chagrin his unfaithful doggy pal completely ignored him and ran up to a Flight Sergeant policeman and licked him to death!

The next morning we set off for Delhi after the AOC had given dear old Desmond his personal farewell at the bottom of the aircraft steps and his grateful thanks to us for taking him! We had flight planned (and had diplomatic clearance) to over-fly Karachi so we allowed Desmond out of his crate to roam as he pleased. He was a lovely dog and he enjoyed his freedom in the aircraft - he came and put his paws either side of the throttle pedestal and occasionally licked our hands! But now the problems began - as we approached Pakistan, Karachi Control ordered us to land at Karachi! Disaster had struck! It would seem our over-flight clearance was denied for some unknown reason so now our illegal passenger could well be discovered without 'papers' and all that that was going to involve with the Pakistani health and customs!

I was greatly concerned at this disturbing turn of events because of our previous experience on the way to the UK over diplomatic clearances at Baghdad! Heaven knows what was going to happen if the Pakistan 'authorities' discovered Desmond without any documentation!

We battened Desmond in his crate and fervently hoped he would keep quiet when the multitude of airfield staff arrived to fumigate and check manifests, (we had none for Karachi which was bad enough on its own without Desmond to contend with!). We sat on the crate with fingers crossed and hoped that no one would want to look in it. Desmond was very good and kept quiet, thank goodness! I hate to think of the bureaucratic and diplomatic complications if they had found him without a manifest, medical documents or even some sort of an animal passport etc. The reception committee overlooked his box in their curiosity at the inside of the strange blue and white military aeroplane that had come so unexpectedly. The two Sergeants remained in the Herald and locked the door while Brian and I went in search of fuel and a new flight clearance. I won't go into the frustration of the next five hours except to say we could not get the Malaysian High Commission to help pay for the fuel and but for the helpfulness of the BOAC Manager in vouchsafing for the cost of the fuel and ground handling charges, we would probably still be there today!

It was with a huge sigh of relief that we got away from Karachi and safely delivered dear old Desmond to the Royal Delhi Hunt. No doubt AVM Johnson was pleased! So far as Desmond was concerned he trotted off happily to his new life in India, without a backward glance or a care in the world!'

When we left Delhi we flew direct to Bangkok - deliberately missing out Calcutta. In my Overseas Ferry Unit days I remembered insuperable problems with the authorities there, in particular with health and paperwork. The Indians seem to be under the impression that visitors brought in all the diseases! Yet whenever I left that city I was always handed a little chit which read something like: *'The health of the city is good - this week only fifty odd people died of Cholera, many of Typhoid'* etc! Dealing with Air Traffic Control was about the same as Karachi! The rest of the ferry back to Kuala Lumpur was uneventful.

The Internet supplied this rather abject photo of a Herald of No.4 Squadron! I remember that it was the occasion when a 20ft python had made its home in the wing!

Chapter 23

CONFRONTATION - BEING SHOT AT DROPPING LEAFLETS

On the 11th April 1965 there was a flurry of secretive activity at the RMAF Base at Kuala Lumpur. I knew something was up, but what? I was told to attend a briefing in the Operations Room at 1800 hrs. There I heard that the RMAF was mounting a leaflet-dropping strike against the Indonesians - Heralds were to fly to the distant targets while Twin Pioneers handled the nearest ones.

I was briefed to drop my leaflets at a known Indonesian terrorist insurgent training camp at Berakit on the northeast coast of Pulau Bintan. I was flying with Flying Officer Brian Love again and also my Malay loadmaster Sgt Syed Mustapha, (who retired as a Major). We had flow many times together and I was happy to know Syed would be in charge of the Army dispatchers down the back.

Intelligence reports stated that there were two or three thousand insurgents at Berakit, which was the place they set out from to raid mainland Malaya.

We took off from Kuala Lumpur (Sempang airfield) at 1.30am and flew 'airways' to Singapore just as if we were on a normal routine flight. We had filed a Flight Plan to Changi and made normal radio calls. On the way down, Syed showed me his great piles of leaflets ready in the fuselage stacked near the rear freight door.

We came off 'Singapore Airways' and called Changi

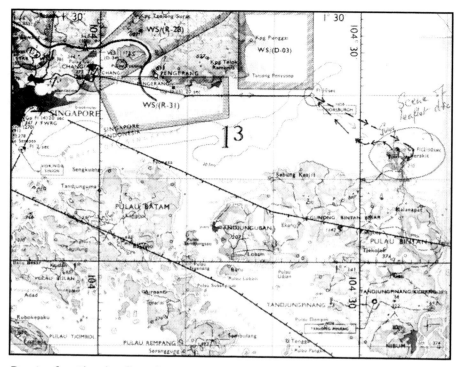

Route for the leaflet drop over Indonesia

'Approach' and commenced a normal approach. We changed frequency to Changi 'Tower' but when we were about to touch down we opened the throttles and climbed ahead. As we did so we blacked everything out, extinguished our Navigation lights, flashing red beacon and all internal fuselage lights. We pretended over the radio that we were taxying in at Changi and called out, 'Shutting down - good night'. Changi ATC went along with this in their replies, as they were 'in the know' about the operation. We did all this in case the Indonesians were monitoring aircraft radio transmissions.

With the Herald in complete darkness and radio silence we set off at low level - about 250 feet - straight to Horsburgh Light NDB (see map). We hoped we would be below any Indonesian radar at that height. At the Horsburgh Light we skirted 200 yards south of it and descended to about 100 feet above the water. This was a bit 'scary' because it is difficult to judge height accurately at night over water but it was a clear moonlit night and ideal for the operation and it also helped us see the ground as we sneaked out to our targets.

We set course for Berakit Peninsular. Syed went off to organise the opening of the rear door and prepare for the drop and we all donned our 'MaeWests'. (We did not have parachutes). Brian Love and I peered out looking for the coastline and the flashing marine light we hoped might be operating on the outline of the coast and adjusted our course to take us towards the headland. I warned Syed down the back to prepare his two dispatchers to be ready to throw out the leaflets (we were using the normal red and green warning lights used for supply dropping). We approached the coast as low as we could and Brian switched on the 'red-on light'. We had been warned at the briefing of the presence of anti-aircraft guns, but no guns opened up probably because we were so very low.

We flashed down the eastern coastline of the Berakit Peninsular about 500 yards out to sea. Our target was about five miles ahead just in from the coast. Even at this hour of the morning there was the odd light about but nothing to give us any clue about the actual location of the target. When we reached about two miles from where we thought the target was, (nothing much could be identified in the jungle background even though it was quite brightly lit by the moon), I pulled up to 500-600 feet and slowed right down to 'dropping speed'. Syed had the door open and his dispatchers were all ready with the leaflet bundles watching for the 'Green On'. I flew now at about 85 knots straight and level peering down to try to identify our drop zone. Brian had been timing on a stopwatch on the run in from the coast and he yelled, 'Now!' and depressed the 'green-on' switch. Syed and the dispatchers started throwing the bundles out and quite a few fluttered back into the fuselage. After about a minute I yelled, 'Stop!' to Syed and Brian switched off the 'green-on' light.

I banked steeply to the left towards the coast accelerating out to sea. As we turned, Brian said over the intercom that he could now see the target and that we had been slightly off it. We hoped the slight wind would at least drift some of the leaflets over that way. I asked Syed how many he had dropped. 'About half,' he replied. I told Brian to keep his eye on the target and I turned sharply over the sea and ran back in preparing to drop again. This time we couldn't miss so I slowed down again to 85 knots. Syed called, 'All gone, Captain!' and I told him to shut the door. I opened up to full power and dived the Herald towards the coastline. So far no one had fired at us as far as we knew, though it was possible that small arms fire could have been aimed at us but we wouldn't have been able to hear or see it unless it hit us.

 Then, just as we passed close to the Berakit Peninsular, heading back for Horsburgh Light, anti-aircraft guns opened up and the coloured tracer lights arched up flashing past us, (just as I remember seeing them during World War II). I dived hard for the surface of the sea and turned our tail on the source of the coloured tracer shells to make a smaller target - many shot past us a little to the side and quite a few above us. I weaved and banked as much as possible to confuse the gunner's radar and hugged the surface of the sea as best I could with its vague moonlit-reflection and headed at full power for Horsburgh Light. I suppose we were being fired at for about two minutes but it seemed an eternity. Those coloured balls of tracer shells, which seemed to start out so lazily and then zip past the aircraft, fascinated Syed and Brian. Luckily we were not hit.

 We stayed right on the surface until we were in sight of the friendly lights of Pengerang on the South Johore coast, heading for the Horsburgh non-directional beacon. About ten miles from Changi, we climbed up, switched on our navigation lights, our beacon light and the aircraft internal lights and called Changi ATC for a normal circuit and landing there. Syed cleared up some of the mess of leaflets and gave me one, which till this day, I have treasured in my logbook here at my home in England.

 I hope that, at least, some of our leaflets landed on target. It would be nice to think they did and maybe had some psychological effect on those who were intent on doing harm to Malaysia. The Herald FM-1027 came through completely unscathed.

Chapter 24

ASYMMETRIC FLAP OVER KUALA LUMPUR

On 21st July 1966, I was teaching a Malaysian co-pilot circuits and landings at Sempang Airport in the suburbs of Kuala Lumpur in Herald FM 1020. The runway in use that day entailed an approach over a very thickly populated area.

After several circuits, he was settled nicely on a final approach at about 400 feet. He called for me to lower full flap and as I moved the flap lever down there was a loud bang and the aircraft started to roll to the left. I could see he was struggling to level the wings and realised something was very wrong, so I yelled, 'I have control,' and grabbed the control spectacle and opened up the throttles to try to overshoot the runway.

In doing so, the roll became more pronounced and the wings continued past 30 degrees of bank. I needed to use both hands, full right rudder and a lot of strength to counteract the roll. I called for the co-pilot to quickly raise the flaps and reduce the power but as we were still losing height and with the control wheel at full deflection and the bank still gradually increasing, it was a case of whether I could maintain some semblance of control to reach the runway or even the airfield if things got worse. However, as the flaps retracted I was able to regain control very slowly, level the aircraft wings and increase a little power. At this point I was convinced the problem was asymmetric flap lowering.

I had to heave back and get the nose up out of the dive and at the same time select full power to ensure we missed the rooftops. We had departed some 40 or 50 degrees from the runway centre line by now and were scraping over the buildings by about 20 feet! It was a very close thing.

I was able to turn back towards the runway and shot straight by the Control Tower at about 50 feet and 20 degrees off the runway heading, much to ATC's astonishment and which prompted a concerned enquiry to know, 'what the hell were we doing?'.

I climbed up to 2000 feet to sort out a plan of action. We realised we had had a very narrow escape - if we had hit the overcrowded tenements it would have been a monumental disaster in which hundreds of people would have been killed, not least ourselves! I called for another aircraft to come up and check if there was any obvious damage (which there was not), so I carried out a slow flying flapless check and made a flapless landing.

Despite vehement denials by Handley Page that it was absolutely impossible for asymmetric flap lowering to occur in the Herald, it was found that the screw mechanism to the flap had broken, through rusting in the humid climate of Malaysia.

I was awarded a Green Endorsement in my Flying Logbook for this incident. The citation read:-

INSTANCES OF EXEPTIONAL FLYING SKILL AND JUDGMENT AT THE RMAF BASE AT KUALA LUMPUR ON 21ST JULY 1966.

On 21st July 1966, Flt Lt N E Rose was giving dual instruction to a student pilot in a Herald aircraft. During a supervised circuit and landing, full flap was lowered at 400ft and 115 knots on the final approach. Shortly after selection of full flap, a bang was heard and the aircraft rolled violently to port.

Flt Lt Rose applied full aileron and starboard rudder but could not stop the roll. An increase of power increased the rate of roll, which indicated asymmetric flap as the possible cause. This had not at first been considered as the manufacturers had stated categorically that due to the design asymmetric flap could not occur.

With the wings nearly vertical, Flt Lt Rose was unable to take his hands off the flying controls and he ordered his student to raise the flaps. This was done and control was eventually regained only a few feet above trees and buildings on the approach.

An overshoot was made and a safe flapless landing carried out. The cause was indeed found to be asymmetric flap caused by a control chain breaking and fracturing the chain guard.

But for the skill, presence of mind and capability of Flt Lt Rose, this technical failure would almost certainly have resulted in the loss of the aircraft and crew. Further, as the incident occurred over a heavily populated area, there could easily have been a dreadful disaster.

Signed:

GEORGE FRAIN
Wing Commander

OC RMAF Kuala Lumpur

20th August 1966

My time was coming to an end and many of the Malaysian members of No.4 Squadron had completed a tour as co-pilots and were rapidly filling the captaincy slots. The way they operated and flew the Herald was mostly through my instruction, and was modeled almost exactly on the way the RAF operated.

Even the social life in the Officers' Mess was modelled on the RAF, including the choice of food. Dining-in Nights and the peculiar games entered into in RAF Messes were enjoyed by the indigenous Malays, Indian and Chinese. Formal dinners at Dining-in Nights were taken in rotation each month for food i.e. Malay, Chinese, Indian and European. It was strange to have these racial menus but equally we all enjoyed each other's food.

My three years seconded to the RMAF were some of the most pleasurable and rewarding times in my 47-year flying career. I obtained enormous job satisfaction helping to mould the squadron pilots and loadmasters of this emergent nation and build them into part of the fine efficient transport squadron it is today. I was given a free hand throughout to introduce and implement all my ideas and therefore shape the flying on the Squadron just the way I wanted to see it done.

Ahli Mangku Negara

The Malaysian Nation honoured me with their *Ahli Mangku Negara*, which is roughly the British equivalent of the Military MBE. They also gave me the *Pingat Peringatan Malaysia* for Services to Malaysia and their *Pingat Perkhidmatan AM* for military operations throughout Confrontation with Indonesia.

I thought very highly of Malaysia and its Malaysian peoples. It was, and still is, is a thriving nation in a lovely

Formal approval had to given for the wearing of the decoration.

176

country and Kuala Lumpur is a lively modern city. I hope one day to return before I die to see if it has changed since I left nearly 40 years ago. My family and I were always treated politely and kindly and we felt no racial tension. We lived in nice houses, had a good social life,

The newspaper cutting reads:
Three members of the RAF were at the Malaysian High Commission last month to receive honours awarded by the King of Malaysia. Air Chief Marshal Sir John Grandy received a Malaysian knighthood which, in Malaysia, would entitle him to be styled Tan Sri (Sir). Flt Lt N E Rose (Brize Norton) and Chief Tech Wheeler received the Malay equivalent of the MBE and BEM respectively. Both had served three years in the RMAF.

good food and were able to swim and enjoy the abundant sunshine. We made lots of friends of the local people. Life was truly good there and I was very sorry to leave.

July 1967 - investiture of the AMN by the Prime Minister of Malaysia, Tunku Abdul Rahman.

Chapter 25

BACK TO BRITANNIAS - TRIBULATIONS OF A 'TRUCKIE'

Prior to my departure from Malaysia the Station Commander had asked me if I would like a recommendation to be posted to the Queen's Flight to fly Andovers, but I had made up my mind I would prefer to fly the brand new VC10s, which were just being introduced into the Royal Air Force. I was granted my wish and I arrived at RAF Brize Norton to attend the fourth VC 10 Course.

I attended ground school with BOAC at Heathrow and did an intense series of sessions in the BOAC VC10 simulator. Back at Brize Norton the RAF topped it all off with another three weeks in the classroom before I eventually began my flying conversion. I went off with my crew on our own on 19th July. The VC10 was a beautiful aeroplane to fly - no vices and easy to land. It was the quietest aeroplane I had ever flown in probably due to the fact that the engines were right at the back. The modern instrumentation, autopilot and electronic aids made it a delight to operate in the air. It used to fascinate me to watch the throttles moving automatically when the automatic pilot was couple to the ILS on an approach. For my final instructional flight on the course I went dual to Hong Kong and back and my final solo trip (without passengers) with my crew was to Singapore and back.

What followed was a slight tragedy in my life. I have always suffered with vertigo - I cannot stand heights. It seems my instructor

Model of the VC10.

on the VC10 had noticed a tendency for me to lean away from the low sill window on the left wall of the cockpit. Because the window was low down it gave me an eerie feeling of 'being too high' (explained by the 'Medics' as a 'low horizon syndrome' whereby a hazy horizon viewed through the low window from great altitude gave the impression of even greater height). This set up a feeling of insecurity - hence leaning away from the window. I was not aware of

leaning away but my crew confirmed it. As a result the powers that be insisted the RAF medical staff looked me over. Once involved with the RAF 'Medics', especially if it is a not too well understood phenomenon, is a long and frustrating business - and it was! I was sent to see the top psychiatrist in the RAF in an endeavour to find out what caused the problem and the whole thing looked like going on for years because there seemed to be no simple answer.

In the meantime I started to instruct in the VC10 Simulator. Then a stroke of luck intervened that I had not anticipated. I was promoted to Squadron Leader and posted to the Britannia Operational Conversion Unit at Lyneham. The 'Medics' were glad to have the problem 'go away' and gave me a restricted medical height limitation of 35,000 feet (which is the maximum height to which the Britannia operated anyway!). I have not flown above that height since, except as a passenger, but it remained on my medical documents for the rest of my career! I was sad not to finish off a tour as a VC10 captain but extremely glad to be out of the 'quacks' hands and back in my favourite Britannia for another tour of flying as a 'Truckie'. As I mentioned previously Long Range Transport crews were affectionately referred to as 'Truckies' (Truck Drivers!) and the following is a cross section of the average life of a 'Truckie' which I extracted from entries in my flying logbooks.

Back at Lyneham once more I did a Britannia flying refresher course with the intention of becoming an instructor on the Britannia OCU. However, I was not too keen to start instructing again and keep going round and round the circuit sat in the right hand seat and rarely handling the aircraft. So I stuck out for another tour as a 'Line' Captain on my old Squadron, No.511, when I had completed the refresher course.

At length it was agreed to let me go back to being a 'line captain'. This time I was a Squadron Leader so it meant I had to serve as a Flight Commander - as well as an aircraft captain. I was given the post of Pilot Leader which entailed seeing that the captains and co-pilots maintained their proficiency standards, received their correct monthly flying and simulator training, were evenly allocated the 'good' and 'bad' route tasks and that the appropriate co-pilots flew with appropriate captains. Last but not least I had to keep wives' morale high by keeping them informed about their husbands late arrivals back etc. - the typical job specification of a Transport Squadron Flight Commander!

But back to route flying - the weather at Gibraltar was usually good i.e. sunshine, no fog, low cloud or much rain but the greatest problem was always the wind round the Rock. If the wind exceeded certain limits a diversion was necessary because it swept round either side of the rock and when it met up again the mixing caused unacceptably severe turbulence. The neighbouring Spanish territory had menacing rockets sited uncomfortably close and it was said they would shoot down any aircraft, which wandered off course into their airspace. Some accurate navigation and close radar control ensured it never happened; but when the aircraft was being thrown around it was hard to keep an accurate course. The very short runway had both ends sticking out into the sea and this made it essential that

'... the immense 2000 feet high Rock of Gibraltar ...'

an accurate touchdown was made right at the start of the runway. As usual with my luck these were the conditions I found on my first ever attempt to land at Gibraltar.

To avoid flying over Spanish territory, the flight path came in to the side of the immense 2000 feet high Rock of Gibraltar ending up with a sharp descending right-hand banked turn around the vertical rock side on to the east approach to the runway. The engineer responded to my constantly changing power requirements hanging grimly on to his four throttle handles. The reassuring voice of the radar controller down in a darkened room in the Air Traffic Control tower kept me on course and away from the dangerously close Spanish airspace. At about 500 feet above the sea the western tip of the runway appeared round the edge of the Rock and the controller's voice began to prepare me for the tight right turn to line me up with the runway.

Gibraltar's runway is very wide compared with normal runways and short for modern jets. The line painted across the runway to warn pilots they must touch down by that point showed up clearly - the penalty for overshooting that line could be a watery and ignominious end by dropping off the far end of the runway straight into the sea! The wideness of the runway also caused a psychological optical illusion, which made pilots think they were visually at the right height to close the throttles, when in fact they were too high, and the violence of the turbulence on the approach also made them keep the speed up for extra control.

Naturally enough I fell into the trap - initially I held off too high then dropped onto the runway a few yards past the warning line and on top of that, going too fast! The flight engineer wasted no time in throwing the propellers into reverse and giving full reverse engine power at my rather urgent request. The end of the runway at Gibraltar always looked much closer than it really was, again due to that optical illusion caused by the wideness of the runway. It took one or two visits under those conditions to get used to it!

There were times in those heady days when I was able to have my family join me in the Britannia. On one occasion I took my wife on the Singapore Slip to spend a few days with friends of ours at Aden. At El Adem the aircraft went unserviceable and we had to night-stop. In our room she spotted the beds were all stood in small cans of paraffin and to her enquiry she was told it was to prevent the local creepy crawlies and bugs climbing into the beds. She didn't sleep a wink!!

When I picked her up on my way back from Singapore at Aden, she experienced the dreaded night double leg via El Adem (described later in this chapter). I never heard another peep out of her about me returning home knackered by drinking and having a 'good time' down the route! Also about this time my son Christopher, as soon as he was old enough, had joined the Wells Cathedral School Combined Cadet Corps and was now equipped with his Air Training Corps uniform so he was able to come to Lyneham and fly with me on continuation training flights. Stood behind me on the flight deck he was able to watch take-offs and landings. Up in the air the co-pilot would let him sit in his seat and take control. However, it did not convince him to follow in Dad's footsteps into the RAF!

Not too many RAF pilots have operated into Lima, Peru. On 22nd September I was heading over the Atlantic via the Azores and Jamaica to Lima. Unfortunately my night stop there was a dismal flop because riots broke out and I was confined to my hotel. Instead, I stood in an upstairs window watching the street fighting. All was quiet by the morning so my crew and I departed to the International Airport to take home RAF ground crews. They had been looking after some RAF Canberra aircraft that were sampling the air over the South Pacific after the French had let off an H-Bomb. As we thundered at full power down the runway on take-off, an engine malfunctioned so the flight engineer yelled, 'Abort' and our spirits rose, as we screeched to a halt, at the thought of another night in Peru. The engine snag was, however, fixed within a few hours and reluctantly we winged our way back to Kingston, Jamaica to refuel.

We then had a super night-stop at Bermuda to make up for Lima . I had a distant cousin there I had not seen for 18 years when she was a diminutive six-year old bridesmaid at my first wedding. I invited her to come to the hotel and have a meal with me. An extremely gorgeous female duly appeared at the appointed time in the hotel lobby at the same time as another RAF crew, also from

Lyneham and who all knew me well, were booking in. I went to meet her and she gave me a warm kiss on the lips witnessed by looks of sheer disbelief by the other crew that a 44-year old like me could 'pull' such a beautiful young girl. Later, when questioned by the curious crew members, I told them it was my cousin and the reaction was, 'Oh yeah! Pull the other one!' My own crew gathered ranks round their gorgeous guest and kept the 'wolves' at bay while we all had a splendid evening together!

In November the Commanding Officer of No.511 Squadron called me into his office and asked me how three weeks as Detachment Commander on Wake Island would 'grab me'. Each year Air Support Command (it had just recently changed its name from Transport Command) exercised its 'Westabout' route for a three or four week period when troops were flown to Singapore and Hong Kong across the Atlantic, Canada, the United States and the Pacific - known as the 'Westabout Route'. At each staging post a transport aircraft captain was put in charge of a staff of operations officers, engineers and movements staff to handle about eight aircraft a day transiting to and fro. It bore the code name that year of Exercise Hosanna. The luckier detachment captains got exotic USAF bases in places like California or Honolulu. I got Wake, which is a very tiny lonely island in the middle of the Pacific Ocean but nevertheless is a very busy transit stop for the USAF military aircraft going to and from the Vietnam War - but could not be called exotic!

The Americans were very friendly and made me and my four officers and 30 airmen very welcome. The little detachment did not have a great deal of time to socialise because the RAF aircraft were coming through 24 hours a day. However, when we could find time we did such American things as go to the bowling alley and eat hot dogs, watch baseball, play the pinball machines, eat ice cream and drink iced tea! Coffee (and iced tea!) was available 24 hours a day in the mess hall and we queued up with the USAF airmen clutching a little card that was punched like a railway ticket for meals - but you could have as much as you could eat each time. At the club called the 'Drifters' Reef' we learned to like Budweiser beer drunk from the can and listen to the jukeboxes playing 'Those were the Days', sung

Britannia captain and crew!

by Mary Hopkins over and over again. The Americans raved about her and played nothing else all day and night. The Americans on Wake Island liked our British sense of humour and joined in the RAF singsongs in the Drifters' Reef in the evenings. . .

Most crews only sleep fitfully and have very little sleep overall. This is a typical example of a slip crews experience from Aden on an inbound flight to the UK (which my wife was given an insight to previously in this chapter). With having to rise at 11 o'clock in the evening for a meal, being tired and irritable was the normal prelude to the final 19-hour crew duty day to come. Inevitably the inbound aircraft would be late getting in from Changi so the outbound crew would find itself sat about dog tired in the hot uncomfortable surroundings. Inevitably also, the incoming slip-crew would probably have a tale of woe about the serviceability of the Britannia they were handing over - known as 'carrying snags' to the crews. Often minor snags had to be fixed causing further delays because the RAF was very sensitive about letting their aircraft fly with any unserviceability other than what was known as 'Fit to Fly'. This often meant crews sat and waited until crew duty time ran out - very frustrating and debilitating to already tired crews as this meant another 15 hours on the ground plus accommodation to be found for fed up passengers as well.

The next problem facing tired crews was the UK weather - snow, ice, low cloud, and fog especially first thing in the morning at the time they would arrive. They had to cope with the teeming London airspace followed by a tricky instrument approach requiring utmost concentration and accurate flying. Then add being dog tired to crosswinds up to the permissible limits, driving rain, slippery icy runways or thick snow were all 'routine' - and maybe finding the cloud base too low after an instrument approach and having to climb away to find a diversion which was fit for landing and, on top of that, probably short of fuel. All everyday items to cope with especially in winter!

I used to climb out of my aircraft in UK after one of these, (scheduled arrival time was 07.10 local UK time), with a dry mouth, abrasive stomach through drinking lousy coffee all night to keep awake and trembling with tiredness. The final straw, of course, would be the 'buggeration factor' of a wretched over zealous Customs official or lack of RAF transport to take the crew from the aircraft.

Arrival at home for the unfortunate crews then usually meant having their ears filled with such things as: 'The car won't start.', 'Mother-in-laws forthcoming visit that morning.', 'the kids have played up.', 'the cooker is U/S.', 'the bills need paying.', 'the electricity is about to be cut off.' and 'why are you so tired you can't listen to me?', and finally... 'I suppose you've been staying up late drinking and having a good time!'. (My wife never said a word again.) Sometimes life for the long-range 'Truckie' could be very cruel and frustrating!

Occasionally non-routine flights went up on the tasking boards in the Squadron operations room, which were not regular schedules down the normal routes, such as VIP flights or even the periodic 'States Trainer'. The object of the States Trainer was to familiarise RAF Transport Crews with operating their aircraft in the environment of the United States and Canada but in particular to give them practice in American procedures at strange airfields. Pilots had to be as slick as the ground controllers to understand their jargon and be utterly 'switched on', because Air Traffic Control was a 'jungle' in the United States. RAF military pilots do not get the constant practice of their civilian counter parts in the USA and so periodic practice to get 'switched on' was very necessary. A more experienced pilot who had been there recently would 'screen' another who had not flown in the United States before.

Thus as part of an ongoing re-familiarisation flight I crossed the North Atlantic to Gander on a 'States Trainer'. Next day we went to Chicago O'Hare, which is the busiest airport in the world. If pilots are slow to respond or fail to understand their instructions instantly they become a danger to other aircraft and flight collisions could occur. Ground control will then reject them and they lose their landing slot. It is simply survival of the alertest. I was nicely settled on an ILS approach into O'Hare in cloud when a huge 747, frighteningly close, slid slowly past me clearly seen in the cloud just off my left wingtip. The 747 was descending on a parallel ILS to the runway alongside the one to which I was descending. The 747's approach speed was faster than the Britannia hence it was slowly passing alongside me. Knowing that other aircraft are making parallel approaches can be very disconcerting and certainly concentrates the mind to listen carefully to the controller's instructions. Accurate instrument flying, interpretation of instructions and particularly approach aid coding is a must.

On another occasion I was taking part in an exercise carrying Vulcan ground crews and their equipment to Fairchild AFB in Washington State. Next morning on the way back to Ottawa the loadmaster came to me to tell me that little balls of mercury were running round in the fuselage! At Fairchild AFB an unserviceable bombing instrument had been loaded for return to the UK and it had obviously broken and the mercury had escaped. Most aeroplanes are constructed with aluminium for lightness and the Britannia was no exception. Mercury attacks aluminium and eats into it, so something had to be done quickly. The aircraft was immediately thoroughly investigated on the ground at the RCAF base at Ottawa. The flight engineer, assisted by the crew, tried to wash the fuselage out with a recommended solution given to them by the Canadians but to no avail. I spent the whole night sending signals and waiting for replies with advice on how the situation should be dealt with. Eventually the engineering staff at HQ RAF Upavon were summoned from their beds to give advice over the 'phone. Already little piles of white powder were appearing where the mercury was getting to work. In the end the Britannia was grounded for almost a week to discover the extent to which the aircraft had been damaged. It was feared the mercury could have run down to the bottom of the fuselage and started to attack places that could cause failure of the pressure hull, which in turn could eventually cause an explosive decompression. This, of course was a very unusual incident but I thought it worthy of a mention.

At times the weather in the United States can be vicious to the extreme. One feature of aviation weather that all pilots fear is freezing rain. The rain falls from warmer air into a layer of freezing air and becomes 'super cooled' i.e. to below 0°C. The super cooled droplets are still in water form as they fall but as soon as they strike anything cold, like an aircraft wing, they freeze solid instantly. Normal anti-icing devices cannot cope with this in the air and it can be a most dangerous hazard indeed.

On this occasion my aircraft was stood on the ground overnight at the United States Air Force base at Offutt in the American Mid-west. When my crew and I went out to our aeroplane in the morning it was cocooned in solid ice, two inches thick! Freezing rain had fallen during the night and now in the morning the temperatures were sub-zero so the ice would not thaw. (When warned in advance by the Met. men the Americans put their aircraft into hangars!). Offutt AFB was a Strategic Air Command base and all hangar-thawing facilities had operational priority for KC135 tankers. The incumbent RAF exchange officer produced baseball bats and told us to break the ice off! It was not a particularly brilliant idea and after a half-hearted attempt that resulted in nothing but aching arms, raw fingers and breathlessness, very little ice was removed!

At lunchtime I became fed up getting nowhere with these antics and retired my crew to the Officers' Club and the Top-3 Club (NCOs) respectively. Since we were in RAF uniform we were of great interest to the assembled Americans in the bar. 'Gee! Are you

British Air Force? Welcome and have a drink!' The Americans are a very hospitable and generous people and they seem to like the British, especially the Royal Air Force. My co-pilot (a handsome rugby playing Welshman), and my navigator and I were wined and dined for the next two days. The co-pilot was a huge success with the USAF female officers with his handsome looks and his superb classical piano playing. One particular young female officer had three medals proudly displayed on her left breast and when asked how long she had been in the Service, told us, 'Three months!' The mind boggles! We were very sorry to leave when a thaw set in after two days and the ice had melted off our aircraft!

A last word about weather hazards - I once flew into a hazardous phenomenon over Turkey, which can be frightening if it is not understood. I was in cloud over the mountain ranges of Turkey, east of Ankara, with the automatic pilot height-lock engaged and flying on an airway, when the airspeed suddenly began to decay off to stalling speed and then just as suddenly built up again to the aircraft Velocity Never Exceed (VNE), the speed above which the aircraft could break up. The outside air temperature also varied similarly. This situation is caused by 'standing waves', which are giant up and down currents caused by an air mass moving rapidly over mountains. The air climbs up over the mountains and descends on the other side and this causes a massive ripple, or wave which travels with the air mass so that as an aeroplane flies into the wave it experiences a large area of down-going or up-going air which in turn slows or accelerates the air relative to the forward inertia of the aircraft. The aircraft's height lock maintains the allotted airway altitude and cannot be changed and so the only thing that can 'give' is the airspeed, so I called for extra power as the airspeed dropped off and at the other end of the scale I had all throttles fully back with no power. The phenomena only lasted for three or four minutes but repeated itself moments later. It certainly frightened me and my crew.

Chapter 26
'AUNTIE FLOW' 1971 - 1973

After two or three years in post most pilots have to move on to allow other pilots to take their place and keep a rotation going. With all rotations there are inevitably some ground posts vacated by someone returning to flying that need to be filled. The posting that awaited me meant being 'grounded' - a thing which all dedicated flyers hate - me especially! I was to become the Senior Flow Controller at Air Support Command Operations Centre (known as ASCOC) at Headquarters Air Support Command at RAF Upavon in Wiltshire. The post of Senior Flow Controller was affectionately known throughout the Transport Fleet as 'Auntie Flow'- this will be explained later.

The job of 'Auntie Flow' was a daunting one. In 1971 - 1972, Air Support Command as it was now known, was a thriving arm of the Royal Air Force. Each day over 100 aircraft could be found winging their way round the world in one place or the other. The Flow Control Cell was the nerve centre of Air Support Command Operations Centre (ASCOC), and it was responsible for the separation and even flow of all aircraft so that congestion was avoided at staging posts around the world. It ensured that all the available facilities for handling aircraft at the overseas bases were efficiently utilised and also entailed detailed forward planning of all RAF aircraft movements throughout the world, all of which had to be plotted in

'... and the day-to-day amendments were juggled on a mammoth wooden computer, ten feet long ...'

advance then rearranged like some gigantic jig-saw puzzle every time there was a delay. The plotting was done on seven gigantic vertically mounted boards covered in graph paper and the day-to-day amendments were juggled on a mammoth wooden computer, ten feet long. Each week some 3000 signals were sifted and actioned and 800 or more aircraft movements planned, plotted and rearranged. Many variables had to be considered within the planning and re-scheduling of every flight, such as crew duty time, crew rest time, slip crew availability, airfield opening and closing times, parking space, fuel availability and passenger accommodation availability - all very critical factors.

This vast responsibility was what I was taking on my shoulders as 'Auntie Flow' (the Senior Flow Controller) and I felt very apprehensive. The Flow Cell operated round the clock, 365 days a year, and was staffed by four Flight Lieutenants (one per shift) who were all, like me, Transport Aircraft captains 'grounded', also much against their wishes! With today's technology the whole thing would probably be handled on one computer by a 'man and a dog' but then it was very much a human function calling for a lot of extremely detailed and meticulous work.

Transport aircraft operations were never predictable. Little local flare-ups, disasters or serious crises anywhere in the world would send ASCOC and 'Auntie Flow' into galvanised activity despatching and flowing transport fleets to anywhere in the world with medical assistance, clothing, tents, troops, tanks, food, vehicles, VIPs etc. Air Support Command's task was to carry anything anywhere at the drop of a hat and was their primary task. Secondary were the scheduled services to all parts of the world in the manner of a civilian airline. Many exercises were also carried out to practise contingency plans to cope with military flare-ups or uprisings. A typical example was the 'Operation Vantage' crisis when I took the first Britannia into Kuwait.

It was RAF policy that aircrew employed in ground appointments should keep their flying currency going with occasional flights. As a result of that policy the Controllers in 'Flow' were given periods of flying to keep their hand in. On one such trip I joined a Belfast crew.

The flight entailed delivering a helicopter to Goa in India. I night stopped there and was accommodated in the Hotel Mondovi in Panjuim. It was instantly obvious that Europeans were a novelty by

The RAF Belfast.

the curious stares from the locals and hotel staff. Only Indian food was available so I was obliged to eat raging hot curry and rice with chapattis! It was the unsympathetic habit of RAF Accountants to always pick the cheapest possible accommodation for the aircrews! Worse was the fact that it was a 'dry' state so I could not even have a beer to wash it down.

That night the monsoon struck with a vengeance and flooded everywhere. It was still pouring with rain when I and the crew departed in the dark at 4 am in a taxi which leaked from every conceivable place while mud was flung up from the muddy tracks through large holes in the rusty floor. Only one dim headlight worked and it was obvious the brakes did not work either! The driver managed to miss fallen trees and trudging Indians by a hair's breadth. The crunch came when we came to the ferry across the river, now a raging torrent. The previous evening the scene had been a picturesque and tranquil scene as the sun was setting while we crossed the river. Now it was a swollen torrent of fast moving muddy water, large logs and fallen trees and other mysterious objects rushing down river in the current. The ferry was a precarious sort of small barge large enough to house about three cars nose to tail and was driven across the river by a small outboard motor guided only by a frayed rope secured on each bank. If the rope broke there was just no way the craft could reach the other bank and would be swept down river. It was a terrifying crossing, everything creaked and groaned and the frail craft strained at the guide rope but it eventually made it! My baggage and I were soaked through by the time we reached the aeroplane.

Fortunately it was hot despite the rain so we all stripped off in the aircraft, put on our dry flying overalls, and rigged an impromptu washing line up in the huge, now empty, freight bay to dry off everything including the contents of our suitcases. We eventually thundered through the rain down the flooded runway sending up a mountain of spray and soon disappeared into the dark grey nimbostratus clouds to lurch and creak our way through the monsoon to Changi, Singapore.

About six months later a task arose to fetch the Victoria Cross and George Cross holders from Australia and New Zealand for one of their bi-annual reunions - this time it was a VC10 which I wangled myself onto.

The sun had just come up as we circled Auckland airport to pick up the New Zealand VCs and GCs. Jack Hinton VC was at the bottom of the steps to meet me. We had met on one of his previous visits to the UK and we were old friends. Jack had kindly invited myself and the crew to his house for a party in the evening to meet Charlie Upham. Charlie was the only living recipient of the VC and Bar. In fact only four men in history have ever been awarded a Bar to the VC. Charlie Upham was a farmer, charming, unassuming and a real gentleman - there is a book written about him called '*The Mark of the Lion*', which tells the story of how this incredibly brave New Zealander won his two VCs in World War II.

Next morning just before take-off, Jack Hinton appeared with a lorry load of beer and spirits for the long trip to the UK. Unless a RAF flight is designated 'VIP', (Very Important People) which means Royalty, Ministers or very Senior Officers, it is forbidden to have alcohol on board. After a hasty consultation it was decided to turn a blind eye and not notice it being loaded!

After a quick stopover at Sydney to pick up some Australian VCs and GCs from there, we landed at Perth to stay the night. Most of the contingent of VCs and GCs joined the crew in the bar that evening so I was privileged to spend a very pleasant time with them. On board now were nine VCs and ten GCs with their families.

Jack Hinton opened his 'bar' on the long haul from Perth to Gan and they were well primed by the time they arrived. Gan had turned out to a man to welcome them and the thoughtful RAF had allowed them a five-hour break for a tour round the island, to relax, swim, eat and talk to the lonely airmen. At about 3 o'clock in the afternoon, Molly (Jack's wife), came up to me with a worried look on her face. 'Norman,' she said, 'Jack's missing - he's been gone since we had lunch in the Officers' Mess.' No one had seen him, but knowing Jack well (he was an ex-Sergeant) I nipped down to the Sergeants' Mess and there he was having a singsong round the piano with the Sergeants. Needless to say Jack continued to dispense his booze all the way to the UK and it was a very happy and noisy band of warriors that emerged down the aircraft steps at RAF Brize Norton.

A bit later on it was decided that the runway at Gan had to be resurfaced and since the job would take three weeks the transport fleet had to land somewhere else between the Middle East and the Far East. All the political and diplomatic necessities were negotiated with Sri Lanka to enable the RAF to stage through Colombo at Bandaranaika International Airport. The plan was to send a detachment from UK consisting of one Squadron Leader in charge (which turned out to be me!), three operations officers, a movement's officer and three ground engineers, plus four airmen from Tactical Communications Wing at RAF Benson to handle the signals. No abatement of the number of aircraft moving to and from the Far East was envisaged so the little detachment had a mammoth task on their hands. They would have to work round the clock and expect to handle four or five aircraft each 24 hours.

I was delighted to be selected to be the Detachment Commander and be shot of my 'Auntie Flow' job for a while. I flew out to Gan on the last VC10 to go through. Subsequently Gan was left with sufficient length of runway at one end to operate a Hercules on 'short field' technique so that Gan was not totally cut off. My detachment flew up to Sri Lanka in the Hercules.

Long-range transport crews are renowned for their indomitable spirit and sense of humour, not least the Hercules crew captained by Flt Lt 'Dick' Barton. They called themselves 'Gan Airline' and used the radio call sign 'GanAir' instead of the normal RAF callsign. The airmen at Gan entered into the spirit of the thing and whitewashed 'Gan Airline' on the side of the aeroplane and considered both the crew and the aeroplane as their own little 'company'! It plied three times per week to Singapore for food rations, beer and mail and twice a week to Colombo. It was also the only means of flying a patient out of Gan in the event of a medical evacuation becoming necessary.

My little detachment at Colombo used to listen out on the due days for the welcome radio call of 'Hallo Colombo, this is GanAir...', which hailed the arrival of our duty free 'grog' and cigarettes from Gan. Prices were pretty steep for such things in Sri Lanka.

Gp Capt 'Cat's Eyes' Cunningham and Peter Bugge, who were ferrying a Trident to China, joined me and a VC10 crew in my room in the Pegasus Reef Hotel, Colombo.

The detachment was accommodated in the Pegasus Reef Hotel about half way between Colombo and the airport. The ride from the hotel was a horrific affair - the taxis had bald tyres, no brakes, lights or springs and all the drivers simply leaned on their horns (when they worked!) and drove like maniacs, swerving round bullock carts and elephants! The roads were in huge potholes and the surfaces consisted of what little there was left of tarmac! When it rained the water splashed up through the rusted taxi floors! Each shift took it in turns amongst themselves not to have to sit in the 'suicide' seat next to the driver at the front travelling to and from work!

Across the other side of the airfield was the Royal Sri Lankan Air Force Base with whom the detachment had magnificent co-operation. One feature worth mentioning was that some of the airmen's married quarters consisted of rows of very old red retired London Transport double-decker buses, suitably renovated and made habitable and reasonably comfortable! These buses were originally bought for use in Colombo City. Some eventually leaned over at amazing angles through broken springs etc, until they were totally

The girls in the coffee bar.

unusable and undriveable. They were then bought up by the military to be converted into two-story married quarters!

At the International Airport, British Airways kindly allowed the detachment to share one of their air-conditioned rooms so the office personnel were able to get some respite from the humid heat whilst they were working, but those that worked within the airport itself were not so lucky! We were accorded extremely generous co-operation from the British Airways Station Manager, a Sri Lankan, and his staff. The local people in Sri Lanka were delightful but would only work at their own pace. I found their fascinating habit of wobbling their head from side to side horizontally and answering 'no problem' when asked to do something could mean either yes, no, or maybe! It looked like 'no' but was meant to be 'yes' but, in fact, usually turned out to be 'maybe'!

The waitresses in the coffee bar at the Pegasus Reef Hotel were most attractive and well educated - they wore a sari with a bare midriff and a small white top, which just covered their breasts. They all had outstanding figures and walked proud and upright as only beautiful Asian women can. They spoke perfect English which would do credit to the BBC. The astounding thing was that they nearly all had nine or ten 'O' levels and some with 'A' levels. Their gracious manners, deportment and infectious sense of humour soon had my detachment airmen drooling over them but such were the old fashioned customs of these predominantly Catholic girls that if they were asked out they had to have a chaperone which soon dampened the airmen's ardour!

However, it was not all work. During what little time we had to ourselves we spent beside the hotel pool or on the beach. I 'organised' a fridge to stock the beer brought up by 'Dick' Barton on 'GanAir' and so no matter what time they came off watch, they could go to my room and have a cold beer or two before going to bed. I 'stood in' on the other officers watches to enable them to have a day off occasionally but mostly I was busy 'trouble shooting' all the

With Ingrid Seneviraine, our assistant with passenger handling. She had ten 'O' Levels and four 'A' Levels and was the daughter of a serving Sri Lankan Air Force officer. Talk about being over qualified!

problems (and there were many!) which cropped up. I was the local ambassador, doctor, paymaster and 'social worker', including convincing the Customs that the crews coming through were not smugglers, (this sometimes meant the crews 'sharing' their cigarettes out!). I handled an imprest of £6000 paying hotel bills, fuel bills, landing charges, taxi fares, and allowances to transit crews when required. I dispensed bandages, aspirins, diarrhoea pills, malaria pills, sticking plasters and ointments and visited, negotiated, cajoled, pleaded and scrounged bits from any one who would listen. I answered all the complaints, comforted the transit crews and kept the local Customs officials sweet! I did not have much sleep in my three weeks in Sri Lana but I enjoyed every minute of it.

On March 24th 'Dick' Barton arrived in the 'GanAir' Hercules last flight to collect the detachment and take us back to Gan. We managed a farewell party in the Pegasus Reef hotel the night before we left to say farewell to all the friends we had made. In some ways I was sad to leave as I had fallen in love with Sri Lanka with its warm climate and friendly people. I had two days off at Gan where the runway was now open once again, then climbed on the first westbound VC10 back to UK to become 'Auntie Flow' once more.

During my two-year tour in Flow Control I had been able to carry out quite a few route flights to keep my hand in - actually a total of 293 hours - more than adequate compensation! My next posting was back to full time flying again and I dearly wanted to return once again to my beloved Britannia's but my superiors wanted me to go to RAF Northolt to fly HS 125s on No.32 (The Royal Squadron). I did not want to do that and despite my protests they would not back down so I decided to apply through a little known Queen's Regulation which permits an officer to return to a previous squadron he had served on. I wrote out my application and much to my surprise it worked! I heaved a sigh of relief and drove out of the gates of RAF Upavon for the last time.

Chapter 27
HONG KONG APPROACHES AND GANDER WEATHER

It was like having a great burden lifted from my shoulders to be back in the left-hand seat of a beautiful Britannia for what will inevitably be my last flying tour. But first it meant the usual refresher course. It is said, and with very good reason, that Royal Air Force pilots are the best trained in the world and not least the pilots of the RAF Transport Fleet who are entrusted with the responsibility of carrying passengers all over the world. Although I already had nearly 3000 hours flying the Britannia it was still required that I should refresh. I had to demonstrate my ability once again to cope with every possible situation and emergency. The Britannia Fleet is rightly extremely proud of its accident free record - only one Britannia was ever lost throughout the 15 years it was flown in the RAF and that was not through aircrew error.

An example of this concentrated refresher training was the final flight - a Global Trainer with a screen crew of instructors and two 'student' crews - involving an eastabout flight right around the world, day and night, in all weathers from ice and snow to tropical thunderstorms, through strange airfields and foreign air traffic control systems spanning an in-flight time of around 75 hours over 15 days. Every possible contingency was practised from ditching drills, fire drills; smoke drills and hi-jacking. The cabin crews were also taught the art of catering, handling 'stroppy senior officers' and coping with heart attacks and explosive decompression. No quarter was given to WRAF Loadmasters who had to show that they could cope with heavy loading work exactly the same as the men.

On Day 5 we flew from Singapore to Hong Kong. Mountains surround Hong Kong airport and when the weather is bad it can be very daunting to the uninitiated. A silly mistake could end up with flying into a mountain. All RAF pilots were screened on the approaches to the Hong Kong runway until they were deemed competent to 'go it alone'. If the weather is good it is pure scenic beauty and luckily on this occasion it was. The most exciting approach is to Runway 15 where the northern end of the runway is embedded in Kowloon city and the other end sticks out into the harbour bay.

I flew down the ILS glide path with only half and eye on the instruments - my attention was riveted on the yellow and white 'chequer board' on the side of a mountain of bare vertical rock directly in front of me. As yet the runway was still out of sight round to the right behind a hill with tall blocks of tenement buildings on it. I continued the descent calling occasionally to my flight engineer to change the power settings. As I came to within half a mile of the chequer board, (to continue on the same heading and descent path would be to fly into its centre), slowly the Kai Tak runway began to appear about 40 degrees to the right. The 20-storey blocks of flats slid past the wing tips and I could almost look up into them as I swung the aircraft round to line up with the runway centre line and dive with full flap down to the end of the runway. The last few hundred yards to the threshold had me almost scraping the tops of teeming overcrowded flats with washing hanging out on long poles. Just under the nose was the overcrowded area called 'Stinkies Market'. The 'flight idle' (throttles closed) call brought the flight engineer slapping all four throttles back as I pulled back on the control column to touch down on the runway, whizzing past the Hong Kong Flying Club on the right. About half way down the runway the water appeared on both sides and to overrun to the end would mean falling off into the Kowloon Harbour!

The Royal Air Force is not a hard taskmaster all the time and so we had the next day off to sample the sights and smells of Hong

Kong. We were fortunate enough to live in the Park Hotel in Kowloon because there was not enough accommodation at RAF Kai Tak, which meant we were right next to the shops and the nightlife! The girlie bars and nightlife of Hong Kong would need another chapter!

On Day 7, loaded to gunnels with Hong Kong 'goodies', we set off across the Pacific to Andersen Air Force Base on Guam. Guam is an island some 2000 miles away from Vietnam from which the USAF operated their B52s bombers over Vietnam. If there was an operational scramble it could mean 'holding off' for some time but we were lucky. I was fascinated to watch the enormous B52s lumbering and roaring noisily into the air while we were refuelling. An hour and half later we were on our way to Honolulu and we crossed the International Date Line and 'gained' a day. The weather was beautiful in the clear blue Pacific sky on our way to Honolulu. . Apart from the sometimes doubtful weather at Gander it was all 'downhill' from now on. A thoughtful RAF had given us two days in Honolulu and another two days in California. The leg into Gander was a night flight and was also a final 'Route Check' where the 'Instructors' became 'Examiners'. As always with me, exam nerves had set in during the previous day when I was supposed to be resting and I had not slept a wink. It turned out to be a classic cliffhanger, the sort all pilots hate even when they are well rested and not being examined. The forecast winds at Gander were gale force and right across the runway and snow was also forecast. During the five hours and forty minutes flight things did not get better. If the winds did not get stronger or the runway ice worse then it was just 'within limits' for crosswinds for the Britannia. With bated breath I listened hard to the crackly Canadian voice reading out the Gander 'actuals' (the actual weather at the time) every half-hour.

The weather got worse so I prepared to go to Goose Bay but that was just about as bad. It has been said that a transport pilot's life consisted of 'hours and hours of boredom interspersed with moments of terror'. Never has a truer word been said. Lady Luck eventually took a hand and the wind obligingly abated a bit and the snow held off. Crosswind landings were not the easiest of landings to accomplish in the Britannia but as I always said 'She's quite a forgiving old lady and provided you treat her with respect and handled her correctly she would not bite!' I made it! The examining team nodded their approval, which meant I could now join my squadron as a fully qualified captain once again. As the student crew with me had also had their route check done at the same time I took them to the bar where we got quietly 'stoned'. The next leg into the UK would be another crew under examination, so we relaxed down the back happy in the knowledge we had all passed and had earned a 'C' category each! We slept like logs all the way to Brize Norton!

Chapter 28
THE PAKISTAN AIR LIFT

'Operation Lucan' was the result of the aftermath of the India-Pakistan conflict when East Pakistan broke away and formed the independent state of Bangladesh. Consequently there was a massive refugee problem, resulting in Pakistanis in Bangladesh wanting to return to West Pakistan and Bangladeshi's in Pakistan wanting to return to their homeland. The fact that India and Pakistan had previously been engaged in open warfare did nothing to help the situation. A glance at the map will show how India divides West Pakistan from Bangladesh (East Pakistan)

I flew out on 24th November to the 'Operation Lucan' detachment in Karachi. Three Britannia's shuttled round the clock to and fro (two each day) from Karachi to Dacca and Chittagong in East Pakistan. The flight took about 4½ hours each way, a round trip of over 4000 miles. Fortunately the weather was reasonable at that time of the year over India so things went reasonably smoothly in the air. The Britannia had seats for 115 but more often than not with infants and children added there were nearer 150 Pakistani souls on board.

Many of these pathetic refugees had probably never seen an aeroplane before, let alone ride in one, and they were confused and frightened. The cabin crews had an appalling time. Most of the passengers were old, ailing, infirm, crippled, incontinent or diseased along with wives and children, all clutching their worldly belongings. They fouled the seats and the aisles and were sick everywhere. Those who managed to go to the aircraft toilets stood on the seats rather than sit on them! But by far the majority did not bother and they just went where they sat! Some tried to brew up and cook in the aircraft aisle or on the luggage using little paraffin stoves! At each turn-round the aircraft had to be hosed out and gallons of disinfectant swabbed around but it did not prevent the stench pervading the aircraft all the time.

Sometimes the hard-pressed and long suffering loadmasters

With my 'Lucan' crew - note the United Nations logo.

were faced with heart attacks or births to cope with. On one occasion a filthy toothless smelly old woman of about 85 became ill and collapsed soon after take-off and not knowing what was wrong with her (no one spoke English), my loadmaster (often a practical joker!) came forward and hammered on the flight deck door. (The crews kept the flight deck door firmly closed to keep out the smell!) With a devilish glint in his eye he told the flight deck crew that he thought the old lady needed mouth-to-mouth resuscitation and would one of the crew help him. Quick as a flash the flight engineer, who knew about the loadie's sense of humour, promptly replied there was a 'flight deck emergency' and no one could be spared and would he kindly shut the door behind him! He departed with a wide grin on his face!

On their days off the crews sat round the swimming pool at the Midway Hotel. We slept in the old BOAC crew hostel but went over to the more salubrious KLM hotel opposite for meals, where the better served civilian aircraft crews lived. The food often left a lot to be desired and the crews periodically went down with ghastly stomach complaints. A rather ghoulish and not uncommon sight on the

Amongst my passengers!

way over to the KLM Hotel for breakfast each morning was to see bodies wrapped in white sheets left outside the hostel for collection in the mornings by the local mortuary service! None of the RAF crews were included, I hasten to say!

The weather was just right in Pakistan at that time of the year for swimming and sunbathing. A Pakistani 'gentleman' came around the swimming pool daily offering to remove verrucas from the hard skin beneath our feet. No one thought they had any until he softened the skin with some sort of potion and then sucked them out with his mouth! A revolting thought and sight but he showed us the tiny white objects about 1/16 of an inch long afterwards. The cost was five rupees (30p) per verucca. It proved quite popular in the end!

The Pakistani beer was almost unpalatable and imported beers cost the earth so the detachment ground crews used their initiative and sent to UK for a giant delivery of home brew beer packs, which was freighted out to them on the next rotation aircraft. They cleaned out some large 44-gallon fuel drums and brewed their own beer! It was powerful stuff and quite definitely an acquired taste! However, it proved much cheaper and had the desired effect - and how!

Just before Christmas my crew and I were replaced and we returned to UK. The three RAF Britannias airlifted over 10,000 refugees (6000 Karachi - Dacca, 4000 Dacca/Chittagong - Karachi) and was quoted as the biggest airlift of human beings ever attempted by the RAF.

Chapter 29
THE GURKHA AIRLIFT FROM HONG KONG

At the beginning of March I flew out to Hong Kong to take charge of an autonomous RAF detachment, known as the 'Britdet' or the Gurkha Airlift. The detachment consisted of two aircraft with ground crew support and three complete aircrews all based at RAF Kai Tak. We were tasked with airlifting Gurkhas to and from Kathmandu in Nepal for eight or nine weeks. Every other morning a Britannia would taxy off the chocks at exactly 9 o'clock with about 100 Gurkhas going home to Nepal. That aircraft would return from Kathmandu the next morning to land back in Hong Kong at around 9 o'clock in the evening.

These magnificent little fighting men from the mountains of Nepal would walk for days down to Kathmandu to join the British Army. They would join for ten or 12 years or even longer and would be sent to Hong Kong or Brunei and sometimes the UK. During their time in service they would send money home to their families and they only saw each other about once every three years when they went on leave to Nepal. A few were able to have their families with them.

Kathmandu was 4000 feet up situated in a bowl surrounded by 12000 feet mountains and was almost inaccessible by air unless the weather was clear. The best weather to avoid the monsoons in Nepal was March to May and September to October. Nowadays Kathmandu is blessed with sophisticated 'let down' aids but in 1974 it had but one Non-Directional Beacon and it was unthinkable to try to get through low clouds into the valley without an accurate precision radar letdown aid. There were 'no-go' times when the weather became very bad with low cloud particularly as the monsoon was approaching and it was therefore necessary to pick up enough fuel at Calcutta to return there if the weather was too bad at Kathmandu. The valley often filled with fog in the early morning and the captains had to take off almost blind and climb very steeply to get above the shallow fog. Every crew had to be 'screened' and shown the way and how to tackle the approach between the mountains and into the valley and the safe way to get out of the fog filled valley in the early mornings.

Soon after I took over the detachment and before the preceding Detachment Commander returned to UK, I set off with a screen captain. We climbed out of Hong Kong on a muggy hot humid morning and set off for Calcutta. The route took us south across the China Sea avoiding the worst parts of the conflict-ridden skies of Vietnam, almost to the northern tip of Malaysia then across the southern tip of South Vietnam, Cambodia, Thailand and Burma and on to Calcutta. The inter-tropical convergence zone was dragging itself and its foul weather northwards behind the sun's zenith so we had the usual fight to avoid the massive towering thunderstorms. The aircraft was always too heavy to climb above the Britannia icing level so we had our share of icing problems, (which have been described in chapter 18). Specifically for the Gurkha airlift, diplomatic clearance had been negotiated with the countries over which they flew and some were highly contentious. Countries such as South Vietnam, Cambodia and Burma were not quite like the usual governments and it was not easy to obtain the clearances. When they were obtained, specific times and heights were stipulated and these had to be strictly adhered to. Any slight variation in timing had to be radioed to the ground control centres of each country. If re-clearances were not obtained for some reason or the aircraft wandered from its cleared route there was a distinct possibility of being shot at especially over those parts of war torn South Vietnam!

Because of a lack of fuel at Kathmandu and also for weather reasons described earlier, each Britannia landed at Calcutta to take on sufficient fuel to reach and land at Kathmandu (without refuelling) and return to Calcutta.

I took off from Calcutta with the screen pilot leaning over my shoulder giving advice. The run into Kathmandu is quite short, about 1½ hours. Once we left the dusty north Indian plain at Simla, the mountains start to rise up to 10,000 feet and above. If the weather is clear, as it was that day, and visibility is good, it is just a question of descending between the mountains down a long valley, which opens up into the bowl of Kathmandu. I was entranced with the beauty of it all - away to the other side of Kathmandu was the snow capped Anapurna range of the Himalayas up to 25,000 feet and beyond to the north east I could see Mount Everest. Twice on later flights, with the permission of Nepal Air Traffic Control, I was cleared after take-off to climb up to 26,000 feet towards Mount Everest and flew as close as possible to the magnificent snow capped peak thousands of feet above me. It was a sight than never failed to take my breath away.

'... *I was entranced with the beauty of it all* ...'

211

In the circuit I was able to look down at the sacred temple of Vishnu at Budhanilkantha (which must not be flown over at any cost!) and at the old but beautiful city of Kathmandu five miles away. In 1974 the single runway at Kathmandu's Tribhuvan Airport was only just long enough to land the Britannia and like Gibraltar it meant touching down exactly at the end of the runway at the correct speed. This was not as easy as it might sound as the ground rose up towards the mountains from the end of the runway so that the big Britannia had to be stood on its wingtip in a fairly tight turn to get round from the downwind leg of the circuit. The final part of the approach was therefore quite steep right down to the touchdown point and required considerable skill on the part of the pilot to heave the aircraft round, get the flaps down and power off, to arrive at the touchdown point correctly and at the right speed.

The screen pilot issued advice and pointed out particular hills or a noticeable building to use as a guide for turning points in the circuit and we went round for a 'dummy' approach and overshoot. On the next circuit the screen pilot kept silent and I sweated my way round, got it just about right, touched down, ordered 'brake dwell' (putting the propeller blades into reverse angles) and 'full reverse' (adding power to the reversed propeller blades) and I disappeared into a cloud of dust. In the dry season the bowl of Kathmandu gets very dusty, as does the runway, so reverse power on the propellers throws dust forward and blanks out visibility. As soon as I felt it safe I cancelled reverse and we shot out of the dust to see sufficient runway left to pull up. It really was an interesting experience and a challenge to pilots of big four-engined aeroplanes. Because it was such a difficult place to fly into, the powers that be decreed that only very experienced captains with proven ability (i.e. held a 'B' Category or above) could operate on the Gurkha Airlift.

Night arrivals into Hong Kong were forbidden to RAF crews except those on the 'Britdet' because bad weather at night could be a worse experience than by day needing skill and experience. The aircraft came and went like clockwork due to the magnificent and untiring efforts of the ground crews who often worked right through the night without demur just to ensure that 'their' aeroplanes left on time.

The 'Britdet' was a proud page in the annals of the history of the 'Whispering Giant'. The *esprit de corps* of the Royal Air Force was never better demonstrated than on the Gurkha Airlift where aircrews and ground crews lived and played together and had their very 'own' aeroplanes to fly and work in an autonomous atmosphere 10,000 miles from home.

My nine weeks as Detachment Commander of the 'Britdet' went far too quickly for my liking. During that time I was able have my wife Dorothy out for a week's visit on what was known as an 'indulgence passage', (a 'freebie' privilege for separated married personnel overseas). I was happy and felt a great sense of achievement - better known as 'job satisfaction' I suppose. Before I went home I was thrown into the RAF Kai Tak swimming pool fully clothed, by the ground crews at a farewell party - to those who do not understand the customs of the RAF it was a measure of their affection! Then the captains of the three crews were also thrown in. I was to return again in September and October but this time, at my request, as a 'Line Captain' so that I could do the flying instead of remaining most of the time on the ground in Hong Kong in the role of the Commanding Officer.

Back again in Hong Kong in September I happily spent the next two months flying to and fro from Hong Kong to Kathmandu. There were good and bad trips through weather, unserviceabilities and sickness. In September the monsoon starts to follow the sun south so we had to contend with the ITCZ across South East Asia, which was beginning to have its fling around Nepal. Almost every early morning take-off from there at that time of year was in the shallow fog in the valley that entailed a climbing turn and a fairly steep circle as soon as I lifted off the runway to ensure I remained close to the proximity of the airfield. (Kathmandu is 4000 feet up and as soon as the sun goes down it cools very rapidly. The air is still quite humid with the tail end of the monsoon so the damp air soon forms into a fog in the bowl. And the colder air high up on the mountain slopes rolls down during the night and also mixes in to become even denser by the morning.). As soon I broke through at about 300 to 400 feet above ground level or so, I could see the hills and was able to continue my turn onto my track and climb up through the valley to Simla, India.

The arrival back in Hong Kong was always a challenge, but even more so at night. Hong Kong by night from the air was a truly magnificent sight; it was like descending into Aladdin's cave illuminated like an overloaded Christmas tree but care had to be taken as the surrounding dark mountains were not visible. When the weather clamped down as it often did then it became a job for only the most skilled and experienced crews. Civil operators such as Cathay Pacific were operating into and out of Hong Kong all the year round, so naturally they were thoroughly familiar with ever facet of the let downs, and also the inherent dangers of the approaches to Kai Tak runway 15. The RAF crews did not have the same experience as the civil operators as they only went there infrequently which was another good reason why only the most experienced crews were selected for the Gurkha Airlift.

The social life was particularly good on the 'Britdet'. During my days off with my crew I browsed round the multitude of shops in Nathan Road, bartered at the stalls in 'Stinkies Market' in Kowloon, went to the fish restaurants at Aberdeen and swam in Repulse Bay. In the evenings we drank the 'San Mig' beer in the RAF Kai Tak Officers' Mess or had the odd evening strolling round the bars of Hong Kong and Kowloon. The WRAC Nursing Sisters invited the crews to parties at the British Military Hospital in Kowloon and in return they were invited to see the lights of Hong Kong from the air when we carried out our night training flights. The officers were often invited to the Sergeants' Mess and many social occasions were arranged with the ground crews around the swimming pool in the evenings.

One weekend my crew and I received an invitation to a curry lunch with the Gurkha Engineers whose men we had been taking to and from Nepal. On the Sunday morning we duly presented ourselves at the Gurkha Officers' Mess at Sekong. It was like a chapter out of a Somerset Maughan novel. We drank ice-cold beer out of pure silver wine goblets first, then had the most magnificent Gurkha curry lunch waited on by the polite Gurkha mess staff. We were entertained by the Gurkha officers and their beautiful and immaculately dressed wives

'... In Kathmandu, the RAF took possession of a delightful red brick building ...'

in the most salubrious surroundings. The thing that impressed me most though, was sitting out after lunch on the Officers' Mess veranda sipping ice-cold liqueurs and beers while watching a pukka polo match! What a wonderful life those British 'Raj' Gurkha Regiment officers had!

In Kathmandu, the RAF took possession of a delightful red brick building with enough bedrooms for each crew member plus the resident Movements Officer and his Sergeant. There was a separate penthouse room at the top known as 'The Captains Cabin' where the aircraft captains always slept! Prior to hiring 'Britannia House', as it was known, we had stayed in local hotels but the accommodation, food and service left a lot to be desired so the British High Commission rented Britannia House. We stocked up in Hong Kong with cases of San Miguel and bottles of Scotch and the loadmaster brought food, which we 'noshed' up in the evening. It was very pleasant to leave behind the humid heat of Hong Kong to spend the night in the cool fresh climate of Kathmandu. Britannia House had a staff of two Nepalese who looked after the crews royally. It was all very pleasant and I looked forward to our night stops there. We were all sorry when it was time to return to the UK.

After 'slipping' at Akrotiri on the way home the Air Movements officer asked me to personally look after a nine-year old little girl named Leanne Jepson who was returning to boarding school in the UK. After take-off I sent for her to come to the flight deck.

'No. 1' and 'No. 2' at Britannia House in Kathmandu

She turned out to be a very sweet and intelligent little girl who sat and chatted confidently to the crew one by one and remained on the flight deck for the rest of the flight to the UK. She took a perspective interest in everything that went on and I was so impressed with her that I took the trouble to write to her parents back in Akrotiri to let them know she had arrived safely back in the UK, and how proud her father must be of her.

Note: - Little Leanne's younger brother became Squadron Leader 'Spike' Jepson who also became the leader of the famous Red Arrows Acrobatic Team in 2003/4.

Chapter 30
THE CYPRUS EMERGENCY

The Turks invaded Northern Cyprus in 1974 as part of a quarrel between Turkey and Greece. I had left UK on 19th July and 'slipped' at Akrotiri in Cyprus awaiting the next flight through to Singapore. I taxyed out at Akrotiri early on the morning of 20th July *en route* to Masirah. Our routing took us out over Nicosia and north into Southern Turkey. Our request for take-off was met with the instruction to 'hold'. After about ten minutes we began to fret but then we were given a 'line up and hold'. 'Stops and props' completed we waited on the runway. The fuselage began to 'stoke up' inside but still Air Traffic held us because they could not obtain our clearance from Nicosia Centre. The Britannia had a very inefficient air conditioning system on the ground so we were hot, perspiring and frustrated by the time we were told to return to dispersal because; 'Paratroops are descending on Nicosia!' Absolutely 'Gob smacked' we taxyed back to dispersal stunned by this piece of information and agog to find out what was going on.

I shudder to think what might have happened if we had gone off over Northern Cyprus and Southern Turkey that morning. We heard later that from 5am that morning Turkish jets had been bombing and strafing north of Nicosia with troops pouring ashore in landing crafts from nine Turkish warships standing off Kyrenia with their guns bristling. There is little doubt we would most probably have been shot down if we had departed!

Everyone spent the day wondering what was going to happen and listened intently to the Forces Radio; they did a really magnificent job keeping everyone appraised of events minute by minute. CFBS (Cyprus Forces Broadcasting Service) gave families detailed instructions on what to do and where to assemble so that the rescue convoys could collect them. The reassuring and unruffled announcers undoubtedly kept the families calm and avoided panic. At one point I well remember an astonishing and dramatic announcement to families in Famagusta: 'Keep your heads down and stay away from windows - Turkish jets are running in from the sea and strafing!'

RAF Akrotiri was a hive of industry and a tower of strength that day, coping with such an extraordinary and unexpected emergency. The full impact of what was happening slowly became apparent. Helicopters of all three Services were dashing in and snatching the frightened and stranded tourists from the beaches along the northern coastline of Cyprus and airlifting them to rescue coordination centres. They made many dramatic rescues. RAF families were evacuated from Limassol and were hosted by the residents of the base Married Quarters. No.2 Officers' Mess was opened up to accommodate the rescued tourists of many nationalities, most of them with only what they stood up in! They were given drinks, food, and blankets to sleep on the floor. Every available person helped out including my crew and we tended those in No.2 Mess till late that night.

Of course, Akrotiri abounded with rumours. Not least was the one about the Keo Brewery being bombed! Stalwart beer drinker's faces became ashen and 'grown men even cried'! Vehement and blood curdling threats were made against the Turkish Air Force! However morale rocketed back up when it became known that it was a maliciously untrue rumour. Fortuitously, beer supplies never faltered throughout the emergency!

By the morning of the 21st, the good old Britannia fleet began trickling in to start a mass evacuation. My crew and I were the first to depart back to the UK and we were allocated 23 French, two Belgian and 60 British tourists, mostly women and children, some still in their bikinis! My crew and I chivalrously dispensed whatever clothing we had and my co-pilot turned up the cabin temperature as high as he could. No sooner had we contacted France Control on our radio than they wanted to know if we had any French Nationals on board so I let one or two of them have a little chat with the French controllers! Immediately France Control cleared us 'direct to Abbeville, (north coast of France), no position reporting required' - instead of having to grind up the French airways reporting all the time. The controllers were profuse with their thanks to the RAF in general, for rescuing their countrymen and flying them home. Towards the end of the flight, one of the French tourists appeared at our flight deck door with a sheet of paper, which had been signed and individually addressed in English with testimonials from each of his fellow countrymen. I still have that piece of paper pasted in my logbook and I quote just a few:

'RAF Forces are the model of organisation and amiability.'
'Thank you for your softly assistance'
'Thank you for your kind assistance - also everybody at Akrotiri.'
'We shall tell our sons what the RAF is'
'Thank you to this crew for taking care of us so kindly.'
'We shall remember the RAF. We all had the opportunity to notice the ability and kindness of the RAF especially to the crew of this flight'

... and many more like - *'Vive le RAF et l'entente cordiale*!'

As Brize Norton runway was being resurfaced we were diverted to Fairford and the refugees were 'bussed' across to Brize. Brize Norton had urgently and efficiently geared itself up for the airlift of a full Britannia every three hours. The logistics and organisation required to transport, receive, document, feed, clothe, accommodate and finally repatriate the thousands rescued from Cyprus was mind boggling - but they did it! The wives, families and Red Cross waited with help and clothing. It was a magnificent voluntary reaction, which did no harm to Anglo-French relations. As for us, we had our 15 hours and were ready to return to Cyprus for another load. The Cyprus Evacuation of 1974 was yet another 'Battle Honour' so to speak, for the Britannia fleet. I cannot recollect the exact total of tourists rescued and evacuated over the ten days it lasted but Britannias were leaving Akrotiri with 100 refugees every three hours, 24 hours a day. The rapid reaction and selfless help of every strata of RAF Akrotiri was simply magnificent. The logistics of the reception facilities were equally staggering at Brize Norton, which was additionally complicated because the aircraft landed at Fairford requiring a complex bus shuttle for the passengers and crews. Just another story of what the Britannia Fleet could do when called upon.

Chapter 31
10,000 HOURS AND FAREWELL TO THE BRITANNIA

On August 28th 1975, returning from Luqa, Malta, in Britannia XM498, I clocked up 10,000 flying hours somewhere over London. At the bottom of the steps at Brize Norton a superb cake with candles and 'Congratulations - 10,000 hours' on it plus a bottle of champagne awaited me. It should have been a happy occasion - my crew joined me back in my room in the Mess and we had a party - but it was, in fact, a very sad moment because I was cruelly informed my flying days were over. It had previously been

The 10,000 hours celebration.

announced that the Britannia fleet was being wound up and the aircraft sold, and I had hoped I would be able to remain at Brize Norton to go out with the last Britannia. Despite promises of this I was told there and then that I was posted to HQ No.1 Group at Bawtry, near Doncaster, to take up duties as an Operations Officer for my last tour of duty before retirement.

The people in the Postings Departments of both HQ 46 Group and the Ministry of Defence were 'at it again'! It had always been understood that, whenever possible, servicemen would be posted as near as possible to the home they had purchased in the area of their choice for their last tour of duty. At 52 I had three years to go to retirement at 55, so earlier in the year I had written my 'formal official' letter asking to be able to serve my last three years as near as possible to my retirement home at Devizes. At no stretch of the imagination could it be said that Doncaster was near Devizes! The whole thing stank! No one could even begin to understand this inept and inhumane piece of posting legislation. I expressed my astonishment but the posting staff would not listen.

The Station Commander at Brize Norton was an understanding and compassionate man who saw my plight as any intelligent person would. He had been my Commanding Officer on 511 Squadron in the past and knew about my troubled marriage and domestic unhappiness, so 'he stuck his neck out' and 'went into bat' on my behalf. The kind Group Captain obviously hit hard and got to grips with the matter because the posting was quashed and diverted to RAF Northolt. He told me he had got into trouble with his superiors! There are not many officers of his calibre who would have 'stuck their neck out' at that turbulent time in the history of the Transport Fleet.

I departed to Gander on September 8th on what was to be my very last flight in a Britannia, taking troops to Calgary for an exercise. I transited through Winnipeg and spent two days at Calgary. I have happy memories there of hiring a huge American car and driving out for the day with my crew to the Banff National Park to see some of the finest scenery in the world.

When I returned to Brize Norton six days later on a Saturday

I now found I had to report for duty as an editor at No.1 Aeronautical Information and Documentation Unit at RAF Northolt on the Monday! It was unbelievable! I had just Sunday and Monday to clear, pack, say goodbye and drive down to Northolt. It was an ignominious and unfeeling end to my 15-year career flying the Britannia. I had served the RAF, and in particular the Britannia fleet, with dignity and honour so I felt it was a very unseemly and unfair way to treat a senior Squadron Leader in this manner.

Even now I had not got much of a deal as Northolt was still 100 miles from my home in Devizes and I would still have to 'Bean Steal' (RAF slang for live in the Mess during the week) as I could not travel that far daily. What is more disgraceful about this whole thing is that when I got to Northolt MOD had 'cocked it up' and I was not needed, as there was no job for me! It is at times like this that I feel ashamed of the way people in the Royal Air Force are treated. On top of that, what hurt more than anything else, was that there was no real need for me to leave Brize Norton at all, as most of the now redundant Britannia aircrews remained there for months until a suitable posting arose for them.

Saddened and disillusioned I arrived at RAF Northolt thinking only a miracle would get me another flying job in the Royal Air Force. After the unceremonious and abrupt manner in which I was bundled off to Northolt one would think my presence there was vital. In fact, as stated, there was no job for me and my arrival out of the blue was an embarrassment to the Commanding Officer of No.1 Aeronautical Information and Documentation Unit (AIDU) to have a Squadron Leader, with greater seniority, hanging about with nothing to do on his unit! My disillusionment turned to fury at this inept and stupid posting.

However, fate took a hand. It must have dawned on MOD that they had 'cocked' up my posting and so I was asked to go out to Colombo at a week's notice to be the RAF's Liaison Officer. I had done the job before and I was only too pleased to go in the light of my unwelcome presence at Northolt.

It was a little different this time - the Government of the day had withdrawn British Forces from the Far East and the Gan Island staging post had been shut down. Despite the rundown, the Hong Kong garrison still existed and the Transport Fleet still had a commitment to a reinforcement task all over the Far East, so it was decided to install a permanent staging post in Colombo.

Thus on 29th December 1975, I stepped off a RAF VC10 at Colombo with a brief to set up a staging post. With the help of one ground engineer I did just that. So, for the next three months VC10s and Hercules flew in and out with no problems, or perhaps it would be more accurate to say that the aircrews and aircraft had no problems! As far as I was concerned the word 'problem' was a vast understatement, as my engineer and I were expected to handle a 24 hour flow of aircraft entirely on our own. I was very lucky if I managed five hour's sleep in a 24 hour period and more often than not the sleep consisted mainly of 'cat naps', taken at odd times during the day or night. The two of us were accommodated in the Pegasus Reef Hotel, a few miles out of Colombo, where I found nothing had changed since I was last there. The journey to and from the airport was just as frightening as before - rust-ridden cars, bald tyres, no brakes, dim headlights, (if any). The hotel problems were still there - regular power failures causing the air conditioning to go off with no water or lights, and what was the most frustrating thing, warm beer in the 'fridges!

There were enormous problems with local administration at the airport. The airport air-conditioning never seemed to work and conditions inside the buildings were hot, sticky and pretty intolerable. Customs, Air Traffic and the airport staff were unaccustomed to RAF methods and quite simply did not cope. All this with just a Squadron Leader and a Chief Technician although we did have local Air Ceylon airport staff to help us!

Many of my signals seemed to be ignored or by-passed by my HQ in the UK and there were times around 4 o'clock in the morning when I would sit down, dog-tired and drenched in sweat and send off a desperate signal (not mincing my words). A typical problem at one time was that a BOAC VC10 was scheduled to arrive at exactly the same time as an RAF VC10 was scheduled out - but the RAF aircraft refused to leave dispersal (where it occupied the stand the incoming VC10 needed) any earlier because it meant it would arrive before Hong Kong opening time - so the BOAC aircraft had to wait on the taxyway until the captain of the RAF one deemed he could leave. Both BOAC and the airfield administrators got very hot under the collar about it and made my life intolerable! I obviously ruffled my senior boss's feathers at HQ with my signalled shots across his bows but eventually he changed the RAF VC10 schedule and it worked. (If I had still been at Upavon as 'Auntie Flow' I could have cured the problem in 30 seconds!) I have the feeling that my name was mud amongst the Air Staff back at HQ Upavon so much so that my efforts in Colombo did not receive any appreciation or thanks. In fact my reception was very frosty upon my return there to make my report!

  Towards the end of my three-month stay in Sri Lanka I managed to get things more organised and was able to enjoy my leisure time and even found time to spend in the hotel swimming pool. By the time I was relieved and left for the UK, the Colombo staging post was a going concern and working smoothly.

  Back again at No.1 AIDU at Northolt, I settled down in the post they had found me and soon took over the job of editor of Terminal Approach Procedure Charts with a staff of two Master Pilots, two Sergeants and an attractive young WRAF called Tina. I led this team for the next two years masterminding a new style of Terminal Approach Procedure charts. The task involved a complete research and re-drawing of every instrument approach chart issued by the AIDU - a massive job not altogether completed by the time I left.

  Life in the Mess was very pleasant at Northolt. It was not the sort of place, being in London, where officers would normally buy houses because of the astronomical prices. Most officers already had their own houses anyway so they left their wives and children and lived in the Mess from Monday to Friday and spent weekends at home. This sort of existence was known by the nickname of 'bean stealing', no charge being made for accommodation or food. The Officers' Mess, therefore, was full during the week and a hectic social life resulted. The aircrews of the resident squadron and the

AIDU staff got on well together so much so that I was able to fly with them quite regularly. It was very much like my early days when that sort of comradeship and *esprit de corps*, so often found in the RAF, helped to make Service life tolerable during enforced separation from our loved ones.

About a year before I was due to retire from the RAF at age 55, I received a letter from the MOD asking me to stay on beyond my retirement date. I accepted on condition I could be posted to A&AEE Boscombe Down, near to my home in Wiltshire, to fly the only remaining RAF Britannia. It was a tongue in cheek gesture and I knew I was being rather cheeky and 'trying it on' but my principles were 'nothing ventured, nothing gained' and 'if you don't ask you don't get'! To my utter astonishment and surprise MOD agreed! (At this time the RAF was short of 200 pilots on its manning requirement, which probably influenced my request in my favour!)

Most of the pilots in a similar position to me did not bother to read the 'small print' when extending their service over the age of 55. They knew the RAF was short of pilots and they were quite prepared to continue serving on the principle, that, overall, the RAF was usually a fair employer.

However, this wasn't the case this time - my last five years of regular extended service was not counted as pensionable, which was very unfair and unjust. I had delivered 42 years pensionable service but got only a pension for 37 years. (I was bitter when I found this out and I have never since found out why regular pensionable service is restricted to 37 years service). Another thing that niggled me was, I later discovered, that Specialist Aircrew did not have their flying pay (about one sixth of their final salary) included as pensionable. They were hard pills to swallow and I changed my mind about the RAF being a fair employer!

However, I was more than happy to be back flying, getting paid for it, and able to live in my own home in Devizes with my wife. My daughter Linda was now living in Hong Kong and my son Christopher was teaching at a school in Rye.

No.511 Squadron, 1975 - split in two! CO 'Tricky'Dicky'!

A farewell model of the RAF Britannia - but 'Hello' to another one ...

Chapter 32

BOSCOMBE DOWN AND TWO 55th BIRTHDAYS - 1979

Events moved fast after my acceptance of extended service and I got my posting to the Aeroplane and Armament Experimental Establishment, Boscombe Down. I went there amazed that a man nearing 55 could actually be returning to flying at that age. It seemed a miracle to me and it seemed my luck was changing at last. I was initially sent to RAF Leeming for a refresher course flying the RAF's latest twin-engined turbo-prop, the Jetstream, before taking up my flying duties at Boscombe Down.

The Jetstream.

Next came a refresher on Boscombe's grand old lady, Britannia XX367. It was the only Britannia left in the RAF and she was painted in the red and white colours of the Ministry of Defence Procurement Executive, MOD(PE). She was used to back up trials on experimental aircraft by positioning all the required ground crews and spares wherever they were needed in overseas locations. Some of the aircraft trials were held in either the coldest or hottest parts of the world so we were lucky enough to be accommodated in exotic hotels in those places. A typical sample of the type of flying was the Polar Certificate in my logbook, which reads:

'*This is to certify that on 21st September 1979 Sqn Ldr N E Rose reached the top of the world and circumnavigated the North Geographic Pole.*'

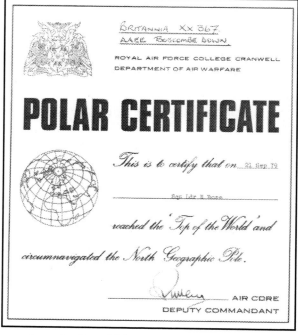

In May 1979 I set off to Woomera, Australia in the Britannia. Whilst in Sydney I had a reunion with an old colleague who had served with me on No.6 Squadron during and just after the war - the person who moved my bed and kit out of my room at Ramat David after my rocket incident! On the 30th May 1979, I celebrated my 55th birthday party with my crew at the Royal Australian Air Force Base at Richmond.

The next morning we took off for Samoa and crossed the

230

A&AEE Britannia at Pago Pago on the occasion of my second 55th birthday!

International Date Line, which turned the date back to 30th May. So, when we landed at the exotic and beautiful island of Pago Pago, it was my 55th birthday again. Much to the unsympathetic cheers of my crew I had to buy the beer for the second time (it is the custom in the RAF that the 'birthday boy' buys the beer!) at my birthday party. I suppose I could be in the Guinness Book of Records again as being the only Squadron Leader to have had two 55th birthdays whilst still flying in the Royal Air Force. (Most officers have to retire from the RAF at the age of 55!)

A&AEE Argosy.

Boscombe Down turned out to be a bit like my earlier days on the Overseas Ferry Unit, i.e. flying many different aircraft types. I flew the Bassett shuttling 'boffins' to and from

One of the Boscombe Down Bassets, XS770, was first used as the training aircraft for HRH The Prince of Wales - two engines are better than one!

aircraft factories, the Argosy on supply dropping trials and the Hercules on trials out on the Aberporth range. It was an interesting and rewarding job for me but I would surely have enjoyed it even more but for the fact that my wife had become ill and my marriage was coming to an end in divorce after nearly 30 years.

On 18th August 1979 my son, Christopher, married Vicki Lelliott (daughter of Vivienne, mentioned in the acknowledgements, who kindly typed up the text of this book). They later made me a proud Grandad with the births of Linda and Christopher in 1951 and 1953.

It was at Boscombe Down,

A Comet 4c was part of the A&AEE fleet, used for the testing of avionic equipment.

flying the Britannia, that I first realised that I was going deaf! Flights over Canada and the USA, where the ground controllers accents were acute, I often could not make out exactly what they said - the crew used to chirp up on the intercom and say, 'Norman, they're calling you!' There is an amusing incident that illustrates this. One day I was going into Honolulu and the controller came up with what sounded like - 'Caution, the rubber end of the runway is slippery.' - but apparently he had said the other end of the runway is slippery! In the end the powers that be sent me to their little hearing cabin and declared me deaf! I was subsequently sent to CME (Central Medical Establishment) in London and I was given hearing aids! (Not worn

Modelling continues! XS766 - another A&AEE Basset.

with a 'bonedome' or headsets, I have to add!) I have worn hearing aids ever since and I am stone deaf nowadays without them.

In 1979, Defence Cuts and financial constraints were beginning to bite at Boscombe Down and the establishment of pilots was being pared down. It was being rumoured that the Britannia's life was approaching its end and that it would go the way of old aircraft - being towed out onto the airfield to be used as a fire and accident training device. I therefore thought it prudent to accept the offer of a job flying Chipmunks as Commanding Officer of No.10 AEF (Air Experience Flight) at RAF Woodvale. I was also keen to be able to leave the Wiltshire area and make a complete break after my forthcoming divorce, which my wife was insisting on, much against medical advice and my wishes. As things turned out, about a year after our divorce and I had left Devizes to go to Woodvale, sadly, my wife died.

Chapter 33
LIFE ON THE AIR EXPERIENCE FLIGHT - 1979-89

I arrived at RAF Woodvale near Southport on 10th December 1979 to become Commanding Officer of No.10 AEF (Air Experience Flight), but I went first, in the New Year, to the Central Flying School at RAF Leeming to refresh on basic flying instruction, as I was now required to instruct on the Chipmunk aircraft.

I settled in back at Woodvale and lived in the Officers' Mess with its basic hutted sleeping quarters, which had changed little since the war ended. My ground crews on the AEF were all civilians and my pilots were also civilians, but held commissions in the RAFVR(T). I was surprised to find the majority of my pilots were

Model of a Chipmunk of No.10 Air Experience Flight.

older than I was and most had very distinguished war records. These VR(T) pilots flew mainly at weekends and many of them travelled over 100 miles return to give ATC cadets air experience flying in the Chipmunks. They had normal weekday civilian jobs as such as dentists, doctors, test pilots, airline pilots, solicitors administrators etc.

I dropped into a routine that was never dull as I was among so many wonderful people from different walks of life who had retired from the RAF with high ranks (even Air Marshals). It was ironic that these highly decorated and experienced ex-service pilots now held ranks lower than mine! Most of them had been flying with the AEF for 20 years or more since they retired from the Royal Air Force, Navy or Army. It was a humbling experience, particularly so as I was obliged to carry out regular flying checks on them called FATs (Flying Ability Tests)!

At the age of 60, in May 1984, I was transferred from the regular Royal Air Force to the RAFVR(T) but maintained continuous service and carried on flying until my 65th birthday on 30th May 1989. I married my new wife, Shirley, on the 26th May 1984 and overnight I 'inherited' four step-daughters/sons with their

A retirement surprise! Self in the cockpit of Gyroflug Speed Canard.

spouses and seven grandchildren!

All 30 of my pilots attended my wedding smartly dressed in their No.1 Uniforms and their wives adorned in all their finery. At the end of the ceremony in the church just before four o'clock, the Padre got very edgy and started to hustle everyone out including Shirley and me who were last. He almost pushed us outside! Little did we know that a prearranged low flypast by a formation of Bulldog aircraft from the two University Air Squadrons at Woodvale had secretly been arranged for four o'clock! With all the AEF pilots lined up on either side of the church entrance, and Shirley and I just emerging, the flypast roared overhead exactly on time! I admit I was so overcome with emotion that I wiped away a tear of pride! It really was a magnificent gesture and an outstanding moment my bride and I will never forget for the rest of our lives. The Padre admitted afterwards that he thought he would never get us all outside in time! There was a splendid reception in the Officers' Mess afterwards!

I finally retired from the Royal Air Force on my 65th birthday, the 30th May 1989, to live with Shirley in Formby. Just before I retired I gained another grandson on 4th April named Tenzin, this time by my daughter Linda who was living in Hong Kong.

With Norris McWhirter and Roy Castle on the presentation of the 1993 book.

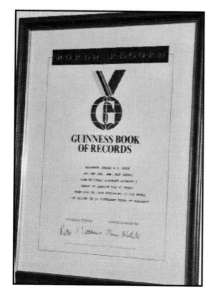

Certificate from the Guinness Book of Records.

Framed display of medals.

As a retirement present from 10 AEF I had the complete surprise of a 50 minute flight in an unbelievable looking little aeroplane called the Gyroflug Speed Canard. It had the most enormous canards on its nose and swept back wings right at the back which were bent upwards two thirds of the way down to become the fins and rudders! It had been flown into Woodvale especially for me by Keith Hartley (who was a BAE experimental test pilot at Warton but also one of my AEF pilots). It was a weird experience as everything was dramatically different in the cockpit - for example everything was in miniature like the tiny little 3-inch control column stalk mounted on the

239

right console! I found myself overcorrecting on this little control and I had only just got the hang of it by the time the flight was over, It was most enjoyable and as a very last flight in my career I felt honoured by it. It was yet another experience I will never forget!

To fill the vacuum of not going to work I set about my hobby of making scale models of every aeroplane I have flown in my 47 years as a RAF pilot. Each of the 72 models is crafted in their authentic colour schemes with the actual airframe registrations and squadron code letters. Many of the photographs in this book are of my models.

When my name was published in the 1993 Guinness Book of Records I was asked by the Imperial War Museum if they could exhibit my models with my flying logbook and medals. After a year or so the whole display was transferred to the Hall of Aviation in the Southampton Museum to form part of their historical archives portraying ex-cadets of the Air Training Corps who went on to have distinguished careers in the Royal Air Force.

In 1999 I was made a 'Master Air Pilot' of the Guild of Air Pilots and Navigators (GAPAN) and I am proud to quote the press release at the time as follows:

'Squadron Leader Norman Rose, who lives in Barkfield Lane, Formby, has been honoured with a prestigious Award by the Guild of Air Pilots and Air Navigators for a lifetime of flying achievements.

'The Award made him a 'Master Air Pilot' of GAPAN. The certificate was signed personally by HRH the Duke of Edinburgh (The Grand Master), and was presented to him on 9th September 1999 at RAF Woodvale. In the 75 years of the existence of GAPAN it was only the 810th to be awarded.

'The criteria of the award is to honour a pilot who has displayed exceptional qualities of pilotage, airmanship and character that has brought honour and respect to the profession and is in recognition of meritorious service in excess of 20 years. The recipient must have shown consistently high standards in professional flying - either civil or military - as a Transport Aircraft Captain, Flying

Instructor, Test Pilot or as an Operational Pilot. Squadron Leader Rose has been all of these during his 47 years and 11,539 hours flying in the RAF which has also earned him a place in the Guinness Book of Records.

'*The Squadron Leader holds the AMN (equivalent to the British Military MBE), one of Malaysia's highest Decorations awarded to him during Confrontation with Indonesia for his services to Malaysia during that war.*

'*He has been decorated twice with Air Force Crosses. The first was awarded in 1957 during the war against the terrorists in Malaya. The second in 1962 for saving a stricken RAF Britannia from crashing into the Indian Ocean halfway between Aden and the tiny island of Gan when a propeller broke loose and put the aircraft in mortal danger. For four and a half hours he struggled just above the wave tops to reach Gan just before the fuel ran out.*

'*He has also been awarded two green endorsements in his flying Log Book for 'Presence of mind, exemplary airmanship and exceptional flying skill and judgement.*'

I am passionately fond of dogs and when not engaged with my modelling, I spent much of my time walking my two Golden Retrievers in the nearby pinewood amongst the red squirrels. Now I also have a little Cavalier King Charles spaniel to walk with.

I am now 82 and have joined the ever decreasing ranks of ex-WW2 RAF 'Coffin Dodgers' but I still glance enviously upwards at the aircraft flying locally from RAF Woodvale and I wish I could have my life all over again. I don't regret a minute of it!

IT SURE AS HELL BEAT WORKING FOR A LIVING!

Appendix 1
SOME PERSONAL PHOTOGRAPHS

Shirley, the intrepid aviator ...

... after a flight in a Chipmunk with me - 1980.

Shirley and I on our way to a Dining-In Night in the Officers' Mess, Woodvale.

Princess Alexandra talking to Shirley at Woodvale - my back to the camera - 26th June 1983.

Coltishall 15 August 1981 - No.6 Squadron reunion with Jack Yates DFM who travelled from Australia.

Duxford 12th July 2003 with KZ321, found in a scrapyard near Haifa, post-war, with ex-No.6 Squadron pilots who served in Palestine.

Britannia Association Reunion 1999. The 'Overspeeding Prop' crew (Chapter 17) reunited. (L to R) Rear: John Beardon (Sig): George Dobson (Nav). Front: Me (Capt): Roy Johnson (Co): Bob Anstee (Flt Eng).

1988 - With the two members of 10 AEF who I recommended, successfully, for the MBE for their outstanding voluntary flying - Harry Knight and Jimmy Reid.

My two 'Goldies' ...

... and my Cavalier King Charles.

Millionth ATC cadet flown at 10 AEF. This cadet became Wg Cdr OC No.13 Squadron.

Air Commodore P V Mayall FBIM RAF — Headquarters Air Cadets
Royal Air Force
Newton
Nottingham
East Bridgford 20771 Ext 401 — NG13 8HR
AC/27390/2/TA

Squadron Leader N E Rose AFC MBIM RAF
35 Barkfield Lane
Freshfield
Formby
Merseyside

16 May 1984

My dear Norman,

Now that you have officially handed over the reins, I should like to record my appreciation of the excellent service you have rendered Air Cadets over the past 4 years. Under your wise command, No 10 AEF has gained a reputation which is second to none. Your dedication to the Air Cadets cause, and your determination to make No 10 AEF a model of safety and efficiency, have been exemplary. I am particularly aware of the sacrifices you have made in recent weeks, to facilitate the takeover of the AEF by your successor.

I am sure you will always gain great satisfaction from knowing that you have been instrumental in giving thousands of cadets their first taste of flying, and in encouraging so many of them to join the next generation of military pilots. I am delighted to note that you will continue the good work as an RAFVR(T) pilot. Congratulations on your forthcoming marriage: and you have my every good wish for a long and happy retirement. Thank you again for all you have done over all the years we have known one another.-

Most sincerely —

Paul Mayall

Letter from the Commandant of Air Cadets on my retirement at the end of my regular service and transfer to the RAFVR(T).

Dining-In Night at RAF Woodvale as OC No.10 AEF, 21st September 1996.

Appendix 2
NOT ALL THE MODEL PHOTOGRAPHS COULD BE INCLUDED IN THE TEXT!

Display at The Imperial War Museum, 1992.

Meteor Mk8.

Buckmaster.

Meteor Mk9.

Beverley - Shawbury MU.

Twin Pioneer at Silloth.

RAF Hercules.

Single Pioneer.

Hunter Mk6.

Hunter Mk7 - two seater.

Meteor NF11.

Meteor NF13.

259